THE 10 COMMANDMENTS

A New Command I Give You,
That You Love One Another

Alex!
You are amazing!
Keep your toes on the
nose and your heart in
heaven! Love,
Max

THE 1~~0~~ COMMANDMENT~~S~~

A New Command I Give You,
That You Love One Another

MAXINE ARMSTRONG

RedeemingPress.com

THE 1 COMMANDMENT
© 2014 by Maxine Armstrong

Published by Redeeming Press
Dallas, OR 97338
RedeemingPress.com

ISBN: 978-1-939992-19-2 (Paperback)
ISBN: 978-1-939992-20-8 (Mobi)
ISBN: 978-1-939992-21-5 (ePub)

For those who are willing

ACKNOWLEDGEMENTS

To my husband, I owe a great big thank you. He endured me asking the same questions *ad infinitum* as I wrote. I could not have done this without his support.

To my children, this book is a hope and prayer that they will not have to unlearn the restraints of religion but be set free to follow the Holy Spirit wherever He leads.

To my Pastor, Terry Miller, who finally convinced me that I was a teacher. Thank you, Terry.

To the Thursday morning Bible study, this is for you. Without you women willing to work it out with joy and frustration and everything in between, we'd never be where we are today. I love you all.

To all my friends and family who came alongside on my journey for a short term or the long haul, your presence in my life has influenced who I am today.

A final and grateful acknowledgement to my publisher, Redeeming Press. Thank you.

TABLE OF CONTENTS

INTRODUCTION

Allow me to introduce myself. I am a lover of Jesus and a lover of the written Word. I have no formal training in the honored halls of seminary. Rather, I identify with the Apostles when it was said of them, "Now as they observed the confidence of Peter and John and understood that they were uneducated and untrained men, they were amazed, and began to recognize them as having been with Jesus" (Acts 4:13). My training comes on the basis of the gifts God has so generously given me, and my communing with Him via the Holy Spirit.

I learn by asking questions, lots of them. I consider unanswered questions a treasure waiting to be discovered. Questions motivate my pursuit of Him. He is the greatest mystery, the most fulfilling love anyone will ever know. I see answers as merely a stepping stone, sometimes small, sometimes large, to the next undiscovered treasure. If you are looking for a book to answer every question raised, or a book that preemptively answers all of its critics, this is not the book for you. If you find yourself wishing I had addressed an issue which I did not, let me encourage you: go on your own treasure hunt with the Holy

Spirit. He will gladly guide you, and you will be rewarded with glory upon glory. Nothing gives me greater joy than discovering truth hidden in plain sight.

The book you now read loosely follows the journey I took in understanding what the Spirit was revealing about the New Covenant. This led to me to find freedom in following Jesus, not rules. After that was worked out, I began quite unexpectedly to see some doctrines in a whole new light. Many of the arguments were worked out from the feedback of brothers and sisters as I shared what the Holy Spirit was showing me. Their questions, objections and encouragements allowed me to seek out an aspect of truth I had not considered. In the process, my understanding was both challenged and refined. Believe me when I tell you that this journey was not easy and came at great personal cost. No matter the cost, I would never go back. Nothing compares to knowing Him. I truly pray what was given me only blesses you abundantly.

As I reflect on the last twenty-plus years of devotion to my Jesus, the non-essentials of my faith have slowly changed. Some new ideas were toyed with for a day and discarded. Others were taken to heart and have become the air I breathe. Do not be afraid of questions. Searching out the answers can be the very thing that deepens your relationship with the living God.

1

THE FATHER WROTE
TWO WILLS

*"This cup which is poured out for you is the
new covenant in My blood." Luke 22:20*

What is the New Covenant? Christians know they are living under a New Covenant, but precious few can articulate what it is precisely. In short, it is both love and freedom, yet flowing from an abiding with the Spirit. Discovering the fullness of this New Covenant will change you forever, if you allow it to do so. Are you ready for a change in perspective? I promise, this is a *most* exciting journey. Although the journey starts in a look at covenants, we won't stay there long, because the ultimate destination is the glory of the freedom we have as the children of God (Rom 8:21). You surely will be challenged. Asking some of the questions and discovering those answers took me to places that rocked my world.

Freedom is not for the faint of heart.

The question: "What is the New Covenant?" captured my imagination one day. Where is it in the Bible? The Old Covenant is plainly seen. Chapter and verses are indisputable, as are the rules and ordinances. The same is true for the covenants God made with Noah, Abraham, and David. Nevertheless, what is the *New* Covenant? Where is it in Scripture? Is it plain to see? If so, what are the rules and ordinances? Initially, nothing came to mind. I somewhat doubted it could be found.

What a joy to be so wrong! So much freedom was waiting to be found. The result of my search is what you now read. I pray you are as blessed as I have been to ask the questions and seek out the answers.

DISCOVERY

The answer to, "What is the New Covenant?" came out of a study in the book of Hebrews, a book that reveals Jesus as the mediator of the New and better Covenant. The beginning of understanding came from these verses:

> For this reason He is the mediator of a new covenant, so that, since a death has taken place for the redemption of the transgressions that were committed under the first covenant, those who have been called may receive the promise of the eternal inheritance. For where a covenant is, there must of necessity be the death of the one who made it. For a covenant is valid only when men are dead, for it is never in force while the one who made it lives. Therefore even the first covenant was not inaugurated without blood (Heb 9:15-18).

The verses were hard to follow and somewhat confusing. Even so, "a covenant is valid only when men are dead … receive the inheritance … there must be the death … only when men are dead …" rolled through my mind on shuffle-repeat.

Two things began to sift through. The first was that a covenant must be a will, because wills are valid when the one who makes it dies. The second was that wills give an inheritance. We will come back to inheritance shortly, but let us start at the very beginning.

COVENANT AND TESTAMENT

There are different sorts of covenants mentioned in the Bible, as well as in our modern day. For example, the marriage covenant is a different sort because it *ceases* to be valid when men die. There has been much study done on extra-biblical Ancient Near East (ANE) covenants. The Code of Hammurabi (1750 BC) is often studied by biblical scholars because it is very much like the Mosaic Covenant. The subject can get multilayered and genuinely intriguing, giving the student a historical context for much study of Genesis and the Old Testament. However, a study in the history of ANE covenants was not the area that drew my attention. The book of Hebrews is a discussion of only two covenants: the "Old" and the "New" (Heb 8:13).

Hebrews looks at the differences and similarities between these two covenants. Namely, the Mosaic covenant, made with the Israelites at Mount Sinai through Moses, and the New Covenant made by Jesus at the Last Supper. Hebrews calls the Mosaic Covenant "the first" (Heb 8:7; 9:1, 18). This is not to disqualify the covenants made prior to the Mosaic, or even afterwards. Rather than disregarding them, Hebrews draws attention to Jeremiah's prophecy of a New Covenant (Jer 31:31), and its fulfillment in Jesus. Hebrews compares and contrasts the Mosaic Covenant with the New Covenant. It is this New Covenant, and how we live within it, that this book explores.

Though we often talk about "covenants" (Old Covenant and New Covenant) and "testaments (Old Testament and New Testament), the words "covenant" and "testament" are outdated and unfamiliar today. Even when they are used, they are used out of context from their original meanings. Most often, the word "testament" describes a section of the Bible, and "covenant" is usually understood to mean a promise. The idea that would not let go of me was that the "covenant" that Hebrews describes is more like a "will." The single word translated into both "covenant" and "testament" is the Greek word *diathēkē*. The first century church would have read *diathēkē* as "will."[1] So "will" is what was meant when written and it is what a reader of Hebrews would have understood. A careful reading of Hebrews leaves little doubt that "will" is the intended meaning.

With this in mind, look again at Hebrews 9:15-18. In the midst of explaining the New Covenant, the author of Hebrews says that death is required before it can be enforced. Just like all wills, the one who made it must die before the heirs get their inheritance.

---

[1] In Classical Greek, *diathēkē* "always meant the disposition which a person makes of his property in prospect of death, i.e., his testament ... (I) A solemn disposition, institution or apportionment of God to man ... (III) Will. There is ample evidence in the papyri that this is the ordinary meaning in the NT. To the Apostle Paul the word meant the same as the Gk. word in the Sept., e.g., a unilateral enactment, in particular a will or testament. ... Undoubtedly in verse seventeen the word *diathēkē* refers to a human will, which becomes a document of value only when the one who prepared it dies. No will is of any value while the one who made it is still alive. The most lucid translation of verse seventeen is that of the NIV: "Because a will [an ordinary will as we know it today and as they knew it then] is in force only when somebody has died; it never takes effect while the one who make it is living." The same meaning of a unilateral will or testament should also be ascribed to Heb. 9:20; 10:29; 13:20, as also in Heb. 7:22; 12:24. The references in Heb. 8:6ff., being mostly quotations from Jer. 31:31-34, use the word *diathēkē*." See Spiros Zodhiates, *The Complete Word Study Dictionary: New Testament* (Chattanooga, TN: AMG, 1993), 424-427.

For where a covenant is, there must of necessity be the death of the one who made it. For a covenant is valid only when men are dead, for it is never in force while the one who made it lives (Heb 9:16-17).

If you replace the outdated word "covenant" with its accurate definition of "will," the meaning is easily understood.

For where a [will] is, there must of necessity be the death of the one who made it. For a [will] is valid only when men are dead, for it is never in force while the one who made it lives.

However, God lives forever. How can an eternal God die to give Abraham or Israel their inheritance? He cannot. Therefore, it had to be done symbolically. The symbolism is seen at Mount Sinai with the blood of bulls and calves. Accordingly, Hebrews affirms the need for a symbolic death in the next verse.

Therefore even the first covenant [will] was not inaugurated without blood. For when every commandment had been spoken by Moses to all the people according to the Law, he took the blood of the calves and the goats, with water and scarlet wool and hyssop, and sprinkled both the book itself and all the people, saying, "This is the blood of the covenant [will] which God commanded you" (Heb 9:18-20).

I had long been taught that God is just and requires a blood sacrifice to remove guilt. But here was a new thing: the text was saying that wills need a death for someone to receive an inheritance. I started to wonder, "Is it perhaps possible that God did not want a 'blood sacrifice' at all?" Upon reflection, it seems it is possible, for Leviticus 17:11 says; "For the life of the flesh is in the blood." Could it be that the sacrifices were a symbolic death *and a celebration of an inheritance received?* Could the picture God was painting for us be one of an "eternal inheritance" rather than the strangely mystical God who demands blood before His anger can be satiated? Asking the questions revealed the discrepancy between the loving Father my heart knew and the misconception of a wrathful Father who still was punishing His children for sins that have already been forgiven.

A CONTRAST OF OLD TESTAMENT COVENANTS

There are all sorts of wills. Some follow certain standards; others, none at all. They are not required to be written an exact way. Even Father God made different kinds of covenants with different people. There are a handful of covenants contained within the Old Testament. We will look at two to see some of the differences. The first example is between God and Abraham. This is called the Abrahamic Covenant. Genesis 15:18 says, "On that day the Lord made a covenant with Abram, saying, 'To your descendants [seed] I have given this land, from the river of Egypt as far as the great river, the river Euphrates.'" It is often said that the Abrahamic Covenant is unconditional. It is not. God did indeed make the promise in Genesis 15 with no requirements. However, God appeared again to Abram and changed his name to Abraham in Genesis 17. At that time God placed one rule on Abraham:

> God said further to Abraham, "Now as for you, you shall keep My covenant, you and your descendants after you throughout their generations. This is My covenant, which you shall keep, between Me and you and your descendants after you: every male among you shall be circumcised. And you shall be circumcised in the flesh of your foreskin, and it shall be the sign of the covenant between Me and you.

And every male among you who is eight days old shall be circumcised throughout your generations, a servant who is born in the house or who is bought with money from any foreigner, who is not of your descendants. A servant who is born in your house or who is bought with your money shall surely be circumcised; thus shall My covenant be in your flesh for an everlasting covenant. But an uncircumcised male who is not circumcised in the flesh of his foreskin, that person shall be cut off from his people; he has broken My covenant" (Gen 17:9-14).

Abraham and all the males in his house were circumcised that "very same day" (v. 23). Once that condition was complete, Abraham became heir to the land.

The next example is the covenant God made with the Israelites at Mount Sinai through Moses. This one had many ordinances and page after page of rules.

See, I am setting before you today a blessing and a curse: the blessing, if you listen to the commandments of the Lord your God, which I am commanding you today; and the curse, if you do not listen to the commandments of the Lord your God, but turn aside from the way which I am commanding you today, by following other gods which you have not known (Deut 11:26-28).

The above can be simply summarized: *If you follow these rules, you will be happy, blessed and live long in the land I am giving you. If you fail to follow these rules, I will curse you and run you out of the land.* Unlike the singular, one-time condition of the Abrahamic Covenant, the Mosaic Covenant had many conditions. The nation of Israel would also gain the land as their inheritance *but only if* they continued to obey all the laws. As a safeguard to prevent the Israelites from breaking those rules, the religious leaders added several thousand more of their own.[2]

Consequently, we see two types of covenants. The Abrahamic had a singular command. Once the condition was fulfilled the covenant was sealed. In contrast the Mosaic Covenant had many conditions and consequently had a performance based outcome (i.e. obedience = blessings, living long in the land; and conversely, disobedience = curses, removal from the land, captivity), because they *agreed* to the conditions.

> So Moses came and called the elders of the people, and set before them all these words which the Lord had commanded him. All the people answered together and said, "All that the Lord has spoken we will do!" And Moses brought back the words of the people to the Lord (Exod 19:7-8).

---

[2] A list of the 613 commands of Torah, can be viewed here: http://www.jewfaq.org/613.htm. Last Accessed January 15, 2014. To this list of 613 laws, the Jewish leaders added thousands of additional laws to put a fence of protection around the law.

Dr. Ron Moseley comments: "The Pharisees counted 613 laws in the Torah, consisting of 248 commands to action and 365 prohibitions. To make sure they did not break even one of these laws by accident or ignorance, they created a hedge around the laws. These hedges are called 'Traditions' in the New Testament. The idea was to establish enough traditions around the Law that an individual would have to break a tradition before he could go all the way to breaking an explicit provision of the Law. Perhaps the best known example of these traditions is the thirty-nine acts prohibited on the Sabbath." Ron Moseley, *Yeshua: A Guide to the Real Jesus and the Original Church* (Clarksville, MD: Messianic Jewish Publishers, 1996), 90.

Ray Vander Laan of www.followtherabbi.com teaches that the "Traditions" and the Talmud came in the wake of the return from the Babylonian captivity. In a desire to keep the law and never fall into the curse of being taken captive by their enemies, the religious leaders created a safeguard for the Jewish people. This safeguard consisted in appointing Sanhedrin, Pharisees and Sadducees, these were a new group of leaders not called for in Torah, whose original purpose was to safeguard, keep and teach the Law.

In contrast, the Abrahamic Covenant had no such curses, and neither does the New Covenant! The New and "better Covenant" does not include curses alongside the "better promises" to those within the covenant (Heb 8:6). We are not under a curse. Period.

DISTRIBUTION OF ASSETS

Though a will is not a law for a populace, it becomes law for the heir if the heir is to receive the inheritance. Abraham stands in contrast to the nation of Israel when it comes to his inheritance. Once circumcised, his inheritance was secured. Alternately, Israel's inheritance was conditional and based on their ability to keep the laws. While our will does not contain curses, it does have "The law of Love." There is one law, to love one another as Jesus has loved us, and one ordinance, to abide in Him. The beauty is that on the occasions we fail to do either, we get *grace instead of a curse!* Much more will be said on this later.

God had promised Abraham he would be a father to many ethnic groups (i.e., nations).

> Therefore, be sure that it is those who are of faith who are sons of Abraham. The Scripture, foreseeing that God would justify the Gentiles by faith, preached the gospel beforehand to Abraham, saying, "All the nations will be blessed in you." So then those who are of faith are blessed with Abraham, the believer (Gal 3:7).

Indeed, he is the father of the Hebrews, but not the Hebrews only. Those of us who are Gentiles are neither of the nation of Israel nor of Moses. However, when we have faith in God we become Abraham's sons and daughters.

Abraham had several sons, but it is the first two upon whom the Bible focuses. The book of Galatians contrasts the first and second born, and tells us these two sons are a prophetic picture. The first son was born to Abraham by Hagar, a slave in his house. The second son was born through a promise from God to Abraham and his wife, Sarah. Galatians explains that the births are prophecy, and compares the sons with the Old and New Covenants. It tells us we also are children of a promise, and therefore free.

> For it is written that Abraham had two sons, one by the bondwoman and one by the free woman. But the son by the bondwoman was born according to the flesh and the son by the free woman through the promise. This is allegorically speaking, for these women are two covenants: one proceeding from Mount Sinai bearing children who are to be slaves; she is Hagar. Now this Hagar is Mount Sinai in Arabia and corresponds to the present Jerusalem, for she is in slavery with her children. But the Jerusalem above is free; she is our mother (Gal 4:22-26).

What does all this mean for us? Are we under the Old Covenant? No, we are under the New Covenant, a new will. We are children born of the promise, born to the free woman, Jerusalem, who is above. We are no longer under the blessings-for-obedience-and-curses-for-disobedience of the old will, because the new will is quite different.

It is not like the old Mosaic Covenant that is based on conditions and performance. Surprising to many, if we are under any covenant found in the Old Testament it is not the Mosaic. Rather, as children of Abraham and belonging to Christ, we are included in the Abrahamic Covenant. "And if you belong to Christ, then you are Abraham's descendants, heirs according to promise" (Gal 3:29).

THE INHERITANCE

If you knew your father wrote more than one will, which one would you be interested in, the older or the most recent? As for me I would want to know all about the last one. I would want to know every stipulation and clause so I could receive my full inheritance, especially if I were the heir to a large estate. Wondrously, there is no estate that is grander. The Kingdom of God is your inheritance.

From the very beginning, our inheritance has been planet Earth. We are told in Romans that Abraham would be heir of the world. In addition to Galatians 3:29 above, Romans 4:13-16 also says our standing in Jesus includes us in Abraham's inheritance:

> For the promise to Abraham or to his descendants that he would be heir of the world was not through the Law, but through the righteousness of faith. For if those who are of the Law are heirs, faith is made void and the promise is nullified; for the Law brings about wrath, but where there is no law, there also is no violation. For this reason it is by faith, in order that it may be in accordance with grace, so that the promise will be guaranteed to all the descendants, not only to those who are of the Law, but also to those who are of the faith of Abraham, who is the father of us all.

The Jews were given exact parameters of their inheritance. However, the Books of the Prophets also speak of a Kingdom. The Old Testament prophets foretell of a future Kingdom in which God vanquishes all His enemies and rules from Heaven and Earth (Isa 9:6-7; Isa 60–61; Jer 15:17-38; Dan 2:44). This Kingdom is our inheritance; it is released with the final will. "Come, you who are blessed of My Father, inherit the kingdom prepared for you from the foundation of the world" (Matt 25:34). The Kingdom is our God-given inheritance and it has been prepared since the foundation of the world. It has always been His plan. Jesus is the mediator of the new and better covenant (Heb 12:24). His death means we have received our inheritance. His resurrected life means we are co-heirs (Rom 8:17) of the Kingdom.

> Then the sovereignty, the dominion and the greatness of all the kingdoms under the whole heaven will be given to the people of the saints of the Highest One; His kingdom will be an everlasting kingdom, and all the dominions will serve and obey Him (Dan 7:27).

WHY WAIT?

The Jews crossed the Jordan River, fought for their Kingdom and actually lived in it. Still, they were waiting for the Messiah who would come, conquer the enemies of God, and take His place in His kingdom. Jesus, the Conquering King, came, and vanquished the enemies of God—namely sin and death—and yet the church still waits for the King and His Kingdom. How can this be? What does this mean? Why must the Kingdom wait until Jesus comes again? It has been a devastating tactic by the enemy to make the Bride (Rev 19:7-9) forget through the centuries where the Kingdom is. She has forgotten the King's throne is in His temple, in the deepest part of His Kingdom. You are the temple of the Living God (1 Cor 3:16). You are in the center of His Kingdom.

Since we know that "without faith it is impossible to please God" (Heb 11:6), let us look to the ancients to see what commendable faith looks like (Heb 11:39). The Hall of Faith starts with Abel, a man of faith who offered a righteous sacrifice. What was it about Abel and his offering? I have heard different valid teachings in my time about how Cain was a sinner (surely he did sin when he killed his brother), followed by a caution to be wary regarding the sin that crouches at our door. Still, the Biblical text does not concern itself with Cain's sin nearly to the degree that it repeatedly affirms Abel's righteousness (Gen 4:4; Matt 23:35; Heb 11:4-6; 12:24). What can be learned from Abel? Hebrews 11:13 tells us, "All these people where still living by faith when they died." "All" being everyone Hebrews has just listed, from Abel to Sarah. I've always thought these people were called faithful simply because they had faith in God, without considering that they also were believing *for* something. The Hall of Faith writer pauses to tell the reader: these Saints were looking forward to *a city in a heavenly country!*

All these people were still living by faith when they died. They did not receive the things promised; they only saw them and welcomed them from a distance, admitting that they were foreigners and strangers on earth. People who say such things show that they are looking for a country of their own. If they had been thinking of the country they had left, they would have had opportunity to return. Instead, they were longing for a better country—a heavenly one. Therefore God is not ashamed to be called their God, for he has prepared a city for them (Heb 11:13-16).

The answer to one of the nagging questions of "Why did God look with favor on Abel's offering?" is found in the verses above. Abel's offering showed he had faith in a coming heavenly country. How? How did the offering of Abel reflect he was longing for a better country? The answer required a little digging.

In the beginning before the Fall, God gave instruction to "rule over the fish of the sea and over the birds of the sky and over every living thing that moves on the earth" (Gen 1:28). It was God's original intent for man to rule over the earth. After the Fall, God cursed the ground, Adam, the serpent and the woman. But, as He always does, God gave hope to mankind. He prophesied that a Child, born to the woman, would crush the serpent's head. Thus indicating a day when man would see victory over the serpent and his dead works.

Eve's children were born into a cursed world, yet a world that had a future hope. There was no time frame given for the promised hope. So Abel, believing in the hope and victory over the serpent, gave heed to the original instruction, "rule over every living thing," and became a keeper of the beasts. Hebrews tells us Abel was longing for a heavenly country. Abel put his faith in the promise of God that "*someday*" could be "*this day*" and lived like it was his "*today*." Abraham believed God when He said Abraham's descendants would be as numerous as the stars, and that he was counted righteous in the basis of his belief (Gen 15:5-6). Abel also believed God for a heavenly country, devoid of the curse, and Abel was also counted as righteous (Heb 11:13-15; Matt 23:35). Abel did not wait for the Kingdom to come to him; he pursued it through faith. In fact, all of the people listed in Hebrews 11 were commended for their faith in "seeking a country of their own ... whose builder and maker is God" (Heb 11:10, 14).

So why wait? The saints in the Hall of Faith didn't wait. Whatever you believe about the Kingdom and your inheritance—that it is here, or here and coming, or still to come—live in pursuit of the promise that it has been given to you. Live in the heavenly country by faith, seeking Him, and you will be rewarded. "Without faith it is impossible to please Him, for he who comes to God must believe that He is and that He is a rewarder of those who seek Him" (Heb 11:6).

HEIRS NOT SINNERS

A common definition of the word "sinner" is "one who misses the mark." Which mark? Perfection? No. Then what? One of the Greek words for sin is *hamartanō*. *Hamartanō* is a negated form of the word *meros*, which means "division, share, portion, allotment." Essentially a sinner is "one who does not have a portion, share, or allotment (i.e., inheritance)." In addition to "one who misses the mark," a sinner is someone who has yet to receive an inheritance. Scripture never calls a believer a sinner. "That is what you some of you were" (1 Cor 6:11). Coming to God in Jesus gives you a new identity, a new name, and a new family. You are no longer a sinner, but a son. "And if a son, then an heir" (Gal 4:7).

However, to not enter into covenant is to continue to remain a "sinner," one who has no share of his Father's inheritance. Of course, even as heirs of God, we all still sin. This does not mean we are not heirs, but that we are not *accessing* the full life afforded to us as an heir within the Kingdom of God.

The prodigal son was willingly given his inheritance while his father was still alive, and the son wasted it. The other son who stayed home never asked for anything. Take a lesson from both sons. On the one hand, do not squander your inheritance. On the other hand, do not live as if you had no inheritance (Luke 15:31).

PASSOVER AND THE NEW COVENANT

Imagine a river as it breaks off into streams and connects back into itself. That is what we will be doing from time to time, since the New Covenant is not solely a will. It is also a wedding proposal, a governmental mandate, and much more. It is not one thing only; the Bible speaks in beautiful imagery and gives many illustrations to capture ideas and concepts. Some examples are: we are the Bride of Christ (Rev 19:7), an army (2 Tim 2:3-4), sheep (John 10:16), and a temple of the Living God (1 Cor 6:19). All are true, but none is the sole truth. So with that in mind let us consider Passover, both the first Passover and the one called the Last Supper.

God had made the covenant with Abraham and his seed, but before the promise was realized Abraham's children would be slaves in Egypt for 400 years. God would then lead them out of Egypt back into the Promised Land with power and wealth. When the time arrived for the children of Abraham, now the size of a small nation, to leave Egypt, God made an additional promise. This time the promise was to Moses and all the Hebrews, saying:

> I have remembered My covenant. Say, therefore, to the sons of Israel, "I am the Lord, and I will bring you out from under the burdens of the Egyptians, and I will deliver you from their bondage. I will also redeem you with an outstretched arm and with great judgments. Then I will take you for My people, and I will be your God; and you shall know that I am the Lord your God, who brought you out from under the burdens of the Egyptians. I will bring you to the land which I swore to give to Abraham, Isaac, and Jacob, and I will give it to you for a possession; I am the Lord" (Exod 6:5-8).

After the Israelites left Egypt, God told them to celebrate Passover every year. He gave the Jews a few instructions on how to celebrate the feast. Between the time of the first Passover and the Last Supper, additional elements and symbolism had been incorporated into the Passover Meal. When God gave instruction for how to celebrate Passover, there was no mention in the Torah regarding the drinking of the cups. The cups, the questions during Seder and the hiding of the matzo are all traditions that came later. Historians think it was a much-loved Rabbi, Hillel the Elder, who contributed much to the Passover

Supper.[3] Since Hillel lived 100 years prior to Jesus, it is believed the Passover Jesus celebrated had many components of a modern day Passover meal. All four Gospel writers include the drinking of the cups as a component of the last Passover. The stories differ slightly, with two common denominators: the cups and the betrayal by Judas. Both the betrayal by a loved one and the cup found their prophetic fulfillments during the Passover Feast.

Today, four (sometimes five) cups of wine are served during the meal. Each cup has a name taken from the promises of Exodus 6. The names differ, but they are generally thus: the first cup is named The Cup of Sanctification and is taken from God's promise in Exodus 6:6a that "I will bring you out"; the second cup is called The Cup of Deliverance and is taken from the promise "I will deliver you" (v. 6b); the third cup is called The Cup of Redemption and points to God's promise that "I will redeem you" (v. 6c); the fourth cup is named The Cup of Hope and reminds those who drink it of God's promise that "I will take you to Me for a people" (v. 7). The occasional fifth cup comes from the promise that "I will bring you into the land" and is also known as Elijah's Cup.

The following is taken from a Jewish website explaining the Seder Dinner:

> 1) There is an open question in the Talmud whether we are obligated to have four or five cups on the night of Passover. Since the issue was never resolved, we pour a fifth cup, but do not drink it.

---

[3] Hillel's contributions to Passover are many as evidenced by the numerous references to his teachings in the Passover section of the Mishnah. However, two specific contributions stand out above the rest: first, the Hillel Sandwich; and second, his teaching that the Paschal sacrifice took precedence over the Sabbath. http://avirtualpassover.com/hillel.htm. Last accessed January 15, 2014.

After heralding the coming of the Messiah, one of Elijah's tasks will be to resolve all hitherto unanswered *halachic* questions. Thus this fifth cup whose status is in doubt is dubbed "Elijah's Cup," in anticipation of the insight he will shed on the matter.

2) The four cups correspond to the four "expressions of re-demption" promised by [God]: "I will take you out from the suffering of Egypt, and I will deliver you from their bondage; I will redeem you with an outstretched arm and with great judgments. I will take you to Myself as a na-tion." *The fifth cup corresponds to the fifth expression of redemption which comes in the following verse: "I will bring you to the Land ..." This expression, however, is an allusion to the future messianic redemption which will be announced by Elijah.* This is also why we do not drink, "enjoy," the fifth cup—as we have not yet experienced this redemption.[4]

Some have presented the Upper Room Passover as a pro-posal of marriage between Jesus and His people. The final cup drunk today is the fourth cup, "I take you for me" which even today is said by the groom to the bride in wedding ceremonies. This is indeed a beautiful picture and fulfills Isaiah's prophecy that they would no longer be called "Desolate" but "Married" (Isa 64:2). Surely this was one of the cups Jesus drank, since Jesus was fulfilling many things that night. He came to fulfill all that was written of Him. Jesus Himself declared that John the Baptist was the "Elijah" who was to come, announcing the Messiah. The fifth cup, which is an unresolved issue and not

---

[4]   http://www.chabad.org/holidays/passover/pesach_cdo/aid/504495/jew
ish/Why-is-Elijah-invited-in-during-the-seder.htm. Last accessed January 15,
2014. Emphasis mine.

drunk today, was fulfilled that night. The cup that celebrates the promise, "I will bring you into the land" was the cup at the end of Supper. Jesus brought us into our inheritance, the Kingdom, when He died. We have received our inheritance. Note carefully three things about this inheritance.

First, "it was not through the Law that Abraham and his seed received the promise that he would be heir of the world, but through the righteousness that comes by faith" (Rom 4:13). Second, "if you belong to Christ, then you are Abraham's seed, and heirs according to the promise" (Gal 3:29). The third, "where a covenant is, there must of necessity be the death of the one who made it, for a covenant is valid only when men are dead, for it is never in force while the one who made it lives" (Heb 9:16-17).

From the very beginning, our inheritance has always been The Kingdom. "Come, you who are blessed of My Father, inherit the kingdom prepared for you from the foundation of the world" (Matt 25:34).

> Think of it this way. If a father dies and leaves an inheritance for his young children, those children are not much better off than slaves until they grow up, even though they actually own everything their father had. They have to obey their guardians until they reach whatever age their father set. And that's the way it was with us before Christ came (Gal 4:1-3 CJB).

God made His New Testament, His "Last Will and Testament" naming us heirs of the world. Jesus made the covenant on the night Israel celebrates freedom from slavery and an exodus into a land that God chose for them. He gave us the two commandments, the clauses of the will: Love one another as I have loved you, and, Abide in Me. Then He went to the cross as the signer of the Testament and died.

Did you know you are the co-owner of a vast inheritance and estate? My friend, your Father made a will and you are His heir. In case no one has ever told you, you are the heir of the world! He owns it all and, amazingly, gave it to you; "the Father, who has qualified us to share in the inheritance of the saints in Light. For He rescued us from the domain of darkness, and transferred us to the kingdom of His beloved Son" (Col 1:12-13).

2

THE FATHER'S LAST WILL AND TESTAMENT

"A new commandment I give to you, that you
love one another, even as I have loved you,
that you also love one another."
John 13:34

Telling someone they have an inheritance waiting for them is easy. Most people will readily accept that news. The next step is far more difficult. Most especially if you grew up in a more conservative vein of Christian thought. The next step requires you to consider something not generally taught, nevertheless I hope to show you through Scripture the truth of it.

Testaments are wills that contain covenants and stipulations to receiving an inheritance. Also, keep in mind we are under a New Testament, with different stipulations than those agreed to with the Old Testament. The new will that our father initiated has a completely new way to get our inheritance; you must comply with the new rules. You cannot win a game of badminton by playing by the rules of tennis, even if they are similar. In the same way, you cannot enter into life and the Kingdom through the rules that "result in sin and death" (cf. Rom 7:9-11). It does not matter how well you play the game or follow the rules.

The Jewish nation was fully aware there would someday be a change of laws. The Jews were in anticipation of this New Covenant ever since Jeremiah had announced some 600 years before Jesus:

> "Behold, days are coming," declares the Lord, "when I will make a new covenant with the house of Israel and with the house of Judah, not like the covenant which I made with their fathers in the day I took them by the hand to bring them out of the land of Egypt, My covenant which they broke, although I was a husband to them," declares the Lord. "But this is the covenant which I will make with the house of Israel after those days," declares the Lord, "I will put My law within them and on their heart I will write it; and I will be their God, and they shall be My people. They will not teach again, each man his neighbor and each man his brother, saying, "Know the Lord," for they will all know Me, from the least of them to the greatest of them," declares the Lord, "for I will forgive their iniquity, and their sin I will remember no more" (Jer 31:31-34).

This passage is repeated again in Hebrews with the added observation, "When He said, "A new covenant," He has made the first obsolete" (Heb 9:13). Even with the knowledge that there is a new covenant, many firmly resist regarding the old as obsolete. For my part, I have not been among a congregation that has fully understood the level of freedom given to the people of God. I have not yet met a body who fully grasp this truth: The Lord will put His laws within us and write them on our hearts. Additionally, there is a certain unwillingness to completely let go of the old because there is good in it. For example, we do not follow the dietary restrictions, or the practice of stoning adulterers, false prophets, disobedient children, or those who practice divination. We do not follow the sacrificial offerings or some of the lesser-known ordinances. However, there are some rules or laws that we do keep, and even protect, because they are considered just and good. In fact, America's laws were based in part on the same laws given at Mount Sinai. The death penalty is based on life for life and is largely accepted as just. As a disciple of Jesus, we would say it is wrong to bear false witness or lie. Honoring Mom and Dad is a good thing. Coveting is frowned upon. Slavery is definitely out even though it was provided for in The Law. The early Christians practiced slavery and slave ownership was common within the churches of the first centuries. The uncomfortable passages regarding slaves and slave owners have been reinterpreted as an employer/employee relationship. Seventh Day Adventists have tried to keep the commandment to honor the Sabbath by gathering on Saturday. Other denominations have chosen to honor the traditions of the early church by fellowshipping on Sunday. The problem is there is no guideline for determining which laws to keep, which to reinterpret and which to throw out entirely. According to the rules under the Old Covenant, we do not have the luxury of picking and choosing which laws we want to follow. *All of it must be obeyed.* Even so, what we choose to follow seems to be based on whether or not it is deemed moral or good in our modern society—and that, too, is currently in flux.

Take into account the Bible agrees that the Law is good. "Take away the disgrace I dread, for your laws are good" (Ps 119:39). Since the Bible says the laws are good; our teaching has strengthened that belief; If our national laws confirm those teachings, and many are in agreement that the law is good (well, at least The Ten Commandments), why not follow the law?

Why not use that which is good—even glorious?

Paul writes in 2 Corinthians about the glory of the Law:

He has made us competent as ministers of a new covenant—not of the letter but of the Spirit; for the letter kills,
but the Spirit gives life. Now if the ministry that brought
death, which was engraved in letters on stone, came with
glory, so that the Israelites could not look steadily at the
face of Moses because of its glory, fading though it was,
will not the ministry of the Spirit be even more glorious? If
the ministry that condemns men is glorious, how much
more glorious is the ministry that brings righteousness! For
what was glorious has no glory now in comparison with the
surpassing glory. And if what was fading away came with
glory, how much greater is the glory of that which lasts!

Therefore, since we have such a hope, we are very bold.
We are not like Moses, who would put a veil over his face
to keep the Israelites from gazing at it while the radiance
was fading away. But their minds were made dull, for to
this day the same veil remains when the old covenant is
read. It has not been removed, because only in Christ is it
taken away. Even to this day when Moses is read, a veil
covers their hearts. But whenever anyone turns to the Lord,
the veil is taken away. Now the Lord is the Spirit, and
where the Spirit of the Lord is, there is freedom. And we,
who with unveiled faces all reflect the Lord's glory, are being transformed into his likeness with ever-increasing glory, which comes from the Lord, who is the Spirit (2 Cor
3:6-18).

Even when it brought death and condemned men, the Old Covenant written on stone *was* glorious. That cannot be denied. So
glorious, in fact, that the Israelites could not even look at the
fading residuals. Who would not want to see the glory as Moses did? Regardless, living in the New Covenant is more glorious. It brings righteousness, life and the power of transformation. Rather than fading over time, the glory continuously

increases as we are transformed into His likeness. Our glory is not like Moses' glory. Moses looked into the law and his glory was fading. We have the abiding Spirit because of the New, and so, our glory is ever increasing. The New Covenant is written by the Holy Spirit, but *not on stone.* Rather, the New Covenant is written in our hearts and minds.

UNVEILED

Why not follow the law? Because we have a new way, a way that brings righteousness and not condemnation. It is superior in every way to the old. Moreover, the Old Covenant was faulty.

Faulty? Yes. Faulty.

How can that be? How could God initiate something that was faulty? I do not have an answer for that, but Scripture declares it true. Scripture declares the Old Covenant to be faulty. Recognizing the fault, God said there was a need for a second covenant, a better one.[5]

> But now Jesus, our High Priest, has been given a ministry that is far superior to the old priesthood, for he is the one who mediates for us a far better covenant with God, based on better promises. If the first covenant had been faultless,

---

[5] Some have proposed that The New Covenant is superior because it was made between God and Jesus and since we are one in Jesus we are included in the New Covenant. I'm fairly simplistic. The Jeremiah prophecy says the New Covenant will be made with "them," and "they" will know Me. On that basis, I believe the New Covenant is made with a plurality of people and not just one person. The NLT seems to be in agreement, since Matthew 26:28 says, "For this is my blood, which confirms the covenant between God and his people." On the other hand, the *Abrahamic Covenant* is between God, Abraham and Jesus (i.e., Abraham's Seed, Gal 3:16) meaning one. It is because we are in Jesus, and one with Him, that causes us to also inherit the promises to Abraham.

there would have been no need for a second covenant to replace it (Heb 8:6-7).

A "far better covenant" and based on better promises too? *What sort of promises*? "If you abide in Me, and My words abide in you, ask whatever you wish, and it will be done for you" (John 15:7). Now, *that is* a better promise! It's undeniably and infinitely better than the old! This better promise was spoken by Jesus at the founding of the New Covenant. Nowhere during this Passover did Jesus say anything even remotely close to, "If you do not obey the Lord your God and do not carefully follow all his commands and decrees I am giving you today, all these curses will come upon you and overtake you" (Deut 8:15). The closest thing in the new to a curse is: "If a man remains in me and I in him, he will bear much fruit; apart from me you can do nothing. If anyone does not remain in me, he is like a branch that is thrown away and withers; such branches are picked up, thrown into the fire and burned" (John 15:5-6).

Nevertheless, even if you are cut off there is still hope of being grafted back in! Romans 11 speaks about the nation of Israel being a cultivated olive branch, which had been cut off for the benefit of the wild olive, which is a picture of the Gentiles. It goes on to say how much more the Lord is able to graft back in the cultivated olive branch. In the same way, He is able to graft back in a branch that was once cut off.

I am not going to study and dissect the word "abide." To ask, "And how do I abide?" reminds me too much of the lawyer who asked Jesus, "And who is my neighbor?" in order to justify himself (Luke 10:25-29). It is far better, I think, to receive it as a daily awareness that I am always with Him and He is always with me. It's more fluid, more relational, and that is the way I like it. I don't need to justify myself to *feel* righteous. I *know I am* righteous because He has made me that way.

TERMS OF THE OLD

Paul makes it very clear; if you try to keep *part* of the old, you are under obligation to keep *all*.

> For as many as are of the works of the Law are under a curse; for it is written, "Cursed is everyone who does not abide by all things written in the book of the law" ... Christ redeemed us from the curse of the Law, having become a curse for us—for it is written, "Cursed is everyone who hangs on a tree"—in order that in Christ Jesus the blessing of Abraham might come to the Gentiles, so that we would receive the promise of the Spirit through faith (Gal 3:10-14).

Knowing the requirement for blessing is based on strict obedience to all the law, read the whole passage from Deuteronomy 28 below (if you can; the list gets downright gruesome). It is a long passage that encompasses curses from the scope of daily living, to curses on your children, to daily sustenance on livestock and the land, to personal disease, to national distress including war and captivity all the way to the eating of your own children and afterbirth. After reading, answer this question: Why would you willingly choose to follow any part of an old, obsolete, faulty, fading, covenant of death which promises to bring curses on you and your children? Why indeed, when there is a better, superior, New Covenant that brings life, righteousness, freedom, ever-increasing glory and the power of transformation?

> But it shall come about, if you do not obey the Lord your God, to observe to do all His commandments and His statutes with which I charge you today, that all these curses will come upon you and overtake you:

Cursed shall you be in the city, and cursed shall you be in the country.

Cursed shall be your basket and your kneading bowl.

Cursed shall be the offspring of your body and the produce of your ground, the increase of your herd and the young of your flock.

Cursed shall you be when you come in, and cursed shall you be when you go out.

The LORD will send upon you curses, confusion, and rebuke, in all you undertake to do, until you are destroyed and until you perish quickly, on account of the evil of your deeds, because you have forsaken Me. The LORD will make the pestilence cling to you until He has consumed you from the land where you are entering to possess it. The LORD will smite you with consumption and with fever and with inflammation and with fiery heat and with the sword and with blight and with mildew, and they will pursue you until you perish. The heaven which is over your head shall be bronze, and the earth which is under you, iron. The LORD will make the rain of your land powder and dust; from heaven it shall come down on you until you are destroyed.

The LORD shall cause you to be defeated before your enemies; you will go out one way against them, but you will flee seven ways before them, and you will be an example of terror to all the kingdoms of the earth. Your carcasses will be food to all birds of the sky and to the beasts of the earth, and there will be no one to frighten them away. The LORD will smite you with the boils of Egypt and with tumors and with the scab and with the itch, from which you cannot be healed. The LORD will smite you with madness and with blindness and with bewilderment of heart; and you will grope at noon, as the blind man gropes in darkness, and you will not prosper in your ways; but you shall only be oppressed and robbed continually, with none to save you.

You shall betroth a wife, but another man will violate her; you shall build a house, but you will not live in it; you shall plant a vineyard, but you will not use its fruit. Your ox shall be slaughtered before your eyes, but you will not eat of it; your donkey shall be torn away from you, and will not be restored to you; your sheep shall be given to your enemies, and you will have none to save you. Your sons and your daughters shall be given to another people, while your eyes look on and yearn for them continually; but there will be nothing you can do. A people whom you do not know shall eat up the produce of your ground and all your labors, and you will never be anything but oppressed and crushed continually. You shall be driven mad by the sight of what you see. The LORD will strike you on the knees and legs with sore boils, from which you cannot be healed, from the sole of your foot to the crown of your head.

The LORD will bring you and your king, whom you set over you, to a nation which neither you nor your fathers have known, and there you shall serve other gods, wood and stone. You shall become a horror, a proverb, and a taunt among all the people where the LORD drives you.

You shall bring out much seed to the field but you will gather in little, for the locust will consume it. You shall plant and cultivate vineyards, but you will neither drink of the wine nor gather the grapes, for the worm will devour them. You shall have olive trees throughout your territory but you will not anoint yourself with the oil, for your olives will drop off. You shall have sons and daughters but they will not be yours, for they will go into captivity. The cricket shall possess all your trees and the produce of your ground.

The alien who is among you shall rise above you higher and higher, but you will go down lower and lower. He shall lend to you, but you will not lend to him; he shall be the head, and you will be the tail.

So all these curses shall come on you and pursue you and overtake you until you are destroyed, because you would not obey the LORD your God by keeping His commandments and His statutes which He commanded you. They shall become a sign and a wonder on you and your descendants forever.

Because you did not serve the LORD your God with joy and a glad heart, for the abundance of all things; therefore you shall serve your enemies whom the LORD will send against you, in hunger, in thirst, in nakedness, and in the lack of all things; and He will put an iron yoke on your neck until He has destroyed you. The LORD will bring a nation against you from afar, from the end of the earth, as the eagle swoops down, a nation whose language you shall not understand, a nation of fierce countenance who will have no respect for the old, nor show favor to the young. Moreover, it shall eat the offspring of your herd and the produce of your ground until you are destroyed, who also leaves you no grain, new wine, or oil, nor the increase of your herd or the young of your flock until they have caused you to perish.

It shall besiege you in all your towns until your high and fortified walls in which you trusted come down throughout your land, and it shall besiege you in all your towns throughout your land which the LORD your God has given you. Then you shall eat the offspring of your own body, the flesh of your sons and of your daughters whom the LORD your God has given you, during the siege and the distress by which your enemy will oppress you. The man who is refined and very delicate among you shall be hostile toward his brother and toward the wife he cherishes and toward the rest of his children who remain, so that he will not give even one of them any of the flesh of his children which he will eat, since he has nothing else left, during the siege and the distress by which your enemy will oppress you in all your towns. The refined and delicate woman among you, who would not venture to set the sole of her foot on the ground for delicateness and refinement, shall be hostile toward the husband she cherishes and toward her son and daughter, and toward her afterbirth which issues from between her legs and toward her children whom she bears; for she will eat them secretly for lack of anything else, during the siege and the distress by which your enemy will oppress you in your towns.

If you are not careful to observe all the words of this law which are written in this book, to fear this honored and awesome name, the LORD your God, then the LORD will bring extraordinary plagues on you and your descendants, even severe and lasting plagues, and miserable and chronic sicknesses. He will bring back on you all the diseases of Egypt of which you were afraid, and they will cling to you. Also every sickness and every plague which, not written in the book of this law, the LORD will bring on you until you are destroyed. Then you shall be left few in number, whereas you were as numerous as the stars of heaven, because you did not obey the LORD your God. It shall come about that as the LORD delighted over you to prosper you, and multiply you, so the LORD will delight over you to make you perish and destroy you; and you will be torn from the land where you are entering to possess it.

Moreover, the LORD will scatter you among all peoples, from one end of the earth to the other end of the earth; and there you shall serve other gods, wood and stone, which you or your fathers have not known. Among those nations you shall find no rest, and there will be no resting place for the sole of your foot; but there the LORD will give you a trembling heart, failing of eyes, and despair of soul. So your life shall hang in doubt before you; and you will be in dread night and day, and shall have no assurance of your life. In the morning you shall say, "Would that it were evening!" And at evening you shall say, "Would that it were morning!" because of the dread of your heart which you dread, and for the sight of your eyes which you will see.

The LORD will bring you back to Egypt in ships, by the way about which I spoke to you, "You will never see it again!" And there you will offer yourselves for sale to your enemies as male and female slaves, but there will be no buyer (Deut 28:15-68).

I can imagine by the time Jeremiah prophesied a new covenant the Jews were heaving a sigh of relief at the thought of walking away from this set of curses.

Since we are living under a New Covenant, again, I ask you: "Why would you willingly choose to follow any part of an old, obsolete, faulty, fading, covenant of death, which promises to bring curses on you and your children?"[6] Why, indeed, when there is a better, superior, New Covenant that brings life, righteousness, freedom, ever increasing glory and the power of transformation?

Galatians 3–5 contain the pleading of Paul *not* to return to the old law but rather to walk by the Spirit. He concludes His plea with: "For the whole Law is fulfilled in one word, in the statement, "You shall love your neighbor as yourself" (Gal 5:14). You may think to yourself, "See there it is, an Old Testament law brought into the New Testament," thus giving validity to our keeping (some of) the Old Covenant. Moved by the Spirit, Jesus lived a life of loving His neighbor as Himself. When He commanded us to "Love one another as I have loved you" He was showing us the full extent of what loving one's neighbor looked like. Jesus had just simplified everything down to the basics. Love God, love one another. Loving your neighbor and loving others in the same manner that Jesus loved people are the same. Paul and John would concur.

> I am writing to remind you, dear friends, that we should love one another. This is not a new commandment, but one we have had from the beginning. Love means doing what God has commanded us, and he has commanded us to love one another, just as you heard from the beginning (1 John 1:5 NLT).

> Let no debt remain outstanding, except the continuing debt to love one another, for whoever loves others has fulfilled the law. The commandments, "You shall not commit adultery," "You shall not murder," "You shall not steal," "You shall not covet, "and whatever other command there may

---

[6] Some of the arguments most often used to justify keeping the law, will be discussed in depth in "Regarding the Law," including Matthew 5:17, "Do not think I have come to abolish the Law."

be, are summed up in this one command: "Love your neighbor as yourself. Love does no harm to a neighbor. Therefore love is the fulfillment of the law (Rom 13:8-10 NIV).

DEAD TO LAW, ALIVE TO LOVE

Let's be honest and admit that we do not even pretend we keep *all* of the law (bacon or tattoos anyone?), but vigorously and robustly defend the keeping of part of it. This is true, even when the Law itself mandates that the whole must be maintained. Part-of or some-of does not measure up when it comes to blessings and curses. When following the law, it is *all* or nothing. Orthodox Jews are very clear on this matter. However, it is not about being Jewish or not. It is about what God said, and God said, "Cursed is everyone who does not abide by *all* things written in the book to perform them" (Gal 3:10).

You probably know of the Old Covenantal rules of stoning the adulterer, false prophet, and even the disobedient child. Further, if they *did not* put these people to death, they were calling down the curse of God on themselves and the nation. The sin of an individual had the ability to apply a curse to the whole. Thus, the law said they *must* execute these people. Not following the law meant national and personal curses. The same holds true for all the other laws in the Old Covenant, from feeding your cattle, to the tithe, to eating shellfish, etc. If not adhered to, curses followed. That is a fearful thought, is it not? It puts a new understanding on what it means to fear God. It also leads to a more compassionate understanding as to why the leaders and Rabbi's made all the extra rules. They didn't love rules- they feared curses and captivity. Aren't you so glad you do not have to live by any of those laws anymore? Once again, we are not under the covenant that pronounces curses on us. On the contrary, we are under grace.

You are not under law, but under grace (Rom 6:14).

Therefore we maintain that a man is justified by faith apart from works of the Law (Rom 3:28).

But if you are led by the Spirit, you are not under the Law (Gal 5:18).

By abolishing in His flesh the enmity, which is the Law of commandments contained in ordinances (Eph 2:15)

Therefore, my brethren, you also were made to die to the Law through the body of Christ, so that you might be joined to another, to Him who was raised from the dead, in order that we might bear fruit for God (Rom 7:4).

When He said, "A new covenant," He has made the first obsolete (Heb 8:13).

Yes, we are under grace; there need not be fear of falling under a curse when we fail. We are not commanded to teach our children to fear the Lord. In 1 John 4:18, we have the oft-quoted phrase, "Perfect love casts out fear." I hear people quote it all the time. It is a good Scripture. However, stopping the verse there is an incomplete thought. Let us look at the larger context.

Dear friends, since God so loved us, we also ought to love one another. No one has ever seen God; but if we love one another, God lives in us and his love is made complete in us. This is how we know that we live in him and he in us: He has given us of his Spirit. And we have seen and testify that the Father has sent his Son to be the Savior of the world. If anyone acknowledges that Jesus is the Son of God, God lives in them and they in God. And so we know and rely on the love God has for us. God is love. Whoever lives in love lives in God, and God in them. This is how love is made complete among us so that we will have confidence on the Day of Judgment: In this world we are like Jesus. There is no fear in love. But perfect love drives out fear, because fear has to do with punishment. The one who fears is not made perfect in love (1 John 4:11-18).

In verse 11, John re-enforces the command, "We ought to love one another." Love is the new command. You will not ever be punished when you abide in love, and the complete knowledge of that releases you from any fear of Him. On the other hand, the Old Testament is filled with the command to fear God. In fact, the Law requires you to fear God (Lev 25:17, among other places). In Deuteronomy alone, it is commanded approximately fourteen times. It is so much a part of the fabric of the Mosaic Covenant that phrases such as "those who feared the Lord" and individuals who were "God-fearing" are synonymous with those who kept Jewish law, both Jews and Gentiles.

Under the New Covenant, the Believer is not given the command to fear God. When the phrase is used in the New Testament, it is used to show someone's relationship to Jewish law. For example, "Now when the meeting of the synagogue had broken up, many of the Jews and of the God-fearing proselytes followed Paul and Barnabas, who, speaking to them, were urging them to continue in the grace of God" (Acts 13:43). The New Testament says to "fear God" just once (1 Pet 2:17). This stands in contrast to the Old Testament, in which several times in the Law and Mosaic Covenant, the people were *commanded* to fear God, and to teach their children to fear the Lord. Consequently, people who obeyed the Old Covenant law were those who were said to fear God. Now, we have been released into Love. Jesus never said, "Fear me" He said, "Follow me." The 1 John verse above affirms we are in God who is Love, as we abide in that place we never need fear. "Because fear has to do with punishment."

We as children of God no longer need fear him. Nor do we need to follow any of the Law of Moses.

I believe the enemy has been trying to drag us back to the covenant of death in every generation. Why do I believe this? Because the question, "Do we have to follow the law of Moses?" is as old as the Christian religion itself. It was answered from the very outset; even so, it continues to be asked in our day. Today the answer is often an uneasily parsed "yes." The answer given at the beginning from the mouth and pen of the Apostles, was a resounding *NO!*

Let's go to Acts 15, trim away the textual commentary and get to the bottom line:

> Some ... of the Pharisees who believed ... [were] saying, "It is necessary to ... direct them to observe the Law of Moses." The apostles and the elders came together to look into this matter. After ... much debate, Peter stood up and said to them, "... why do you put God to the test by placing upon the neck of the disciples a yoke which neither our fathers nor we have been able to bear? ... James answered, saying, "... It is my judgment that we do not trouble those who are turning to God from among the Gentiles, but that we write to them that they abstain from things contaminated by idols and from fornication and from what is strangled and from blood." ... Then it seemed good to the apostles and the elders, with the whole church ... and they sent this letter ... "For it seemed good to the Holy Spirit and to us to lay upon you no greater burden than these essentials: that you abstain from things sacrificed to idols and from blood and from things strangled and from fornication; if you keep yourselves free from such things, you will do well. Farewell" (Acts 15:5-29).

The Apostles, led by the Holy Spirit, determined Gentile believers did not have to follow the laws and ordinances given to
Moses. It seems the first-century Jews were also in agreement
with the fact that this "new sect" (Acts 24:14) was not following the laws. In fact, the Jews were ready to kill Paul for that
very reason. Here is the testimony of the Jews against Paul,
"Fellow Israelites, help us! This is the man who teaches everyone everywhere against our people and our law and this place"
(Acts 21:28). The Jews were under no illusion that those who
professed Jesus were following Jewish law. On the contrary,
they were absolutely certain they were *not*.

Am I really saying the law is not even supposed to be at-
tempted to be followed? Yes. But I am only saying what the
Bible says. Am I saying there are *no* set rules of conduct? Do I
really believe I can do *anything* I want because I am not required to follow certain laws? Of course not, silly! On the other
hand, *yes*! Paul said, "All things are lawful" (1 Cor 10:23). It
doesn't matter whether Paul meant that as a rhetorical argument or a statement of fact. Because when we are abiding with
Him, our heart's desire becomes His heart's desire.

Alright, you are torn, correct? I know you are, as I have had
this conversation enough times to know what you are likely to
be thinking. The objection is very often, "But the Law is a tutor
to lead us to Christ!" If you are like most people, at this point,
you are wrestling with what you have been taught and the light
of freedom that is already beginning to shine. You still want
answers that satisfy your objections, correct? Of course you do.
I asked the same question. I will address the Law as our tutor
later, in the chapter, *Regarding the Law*. First, we will ask,
"What is the New Covenant?" Alternately, some may wish to
skip to the chapter titled, *Regarding the Law*, I trust it will answer any lingering objections that favor keeping the law.

3

WHAT IS THE
NEW COVENANT?

*"But now we have been released from the law,
for we died to it and are no longer captive to
its power. Now we can serve God, not in the
old way of obeying the letter of the law, but in
the new way of living in the Spirit."*
Romans 7:6 NLT

Right about now you may be thinking, "There must be a law,
there must be *some* guideline for living!"

Okay, you are right. There is.

Do you feel better?

Would you like to know what it is? Well, that is the key to
understanding the whole New Covenant. Aside from loving
like Jesus and abiding in Him, I cannot really tell you. Only the
Holy Spirit can. You have undoubtedly heard, "It's not a religion, it's a relationship." The Holy Spirit is the "Who" who
turns Christianity from a religion into a relationship with God.
Allow me to explain. You will love it, if you love Jesus and
value relationship with Him.

SO THE WORLD WILL KNOW

The covenants God made with His children were as much for his children as the rest of the world. God wanted those outside the covenants to be drawn into covenant with Him, because the covenants were so appealing. It is true that Jesus wasn't appealing to everyone. But even those who didn't like Him jealously acknowledged the populace's great attraction to Jesus, even after He left the earth.

> Paul ... went to them, and ... reasoned with them ... saying, "This Jesus whom I am proclaiming to you is the Christ." Some were persuaded and joined Paul and Silas, along with a large number of the God-fearing Greeks and a number of the leading women. But the Jews, becoming jealous and taking along some wicked men from the market place, formed a mob and set the city in an uproar ... shouting, "These men who have upset the world have come here also" (Acts 17:1-7).

All evidence points to the fact that the Apostles and early disciples were living out the New Covenant in a way that created the results Jesus said it would. "Love one another, even as I have loved you ... By this all men will know that you are My disciples, if you have love for one another" (John 13:34-35).

The imagery of the Old and New Covenants have many parallels. Following Jesus is supposed to be lived out in a way that others want to follow Him. Abiding in Him, asking and receiving from Him, would make others say that God is so near to us that He answers whenever we call. When Israel received the Law at Sinai, one of the intents was the world would look at the Jewish nation and know simply by their laws that there was something special about them. It would be evident because their laws were more righteous than those of other nations.

See, I have taught you statutes and judgments just as the Lord my God commanded me, that you should do thus in the land where you are entering to possess it. So keep and do them, for that is your wisdom and your understanding in the sight of the peoples who will hear all these statutes and say, "Surely this great nation is a wise and understanding people." For what great nation is there that has a god so near to it as is the Lord our God whenever we call on Him? Or what great nation is there that has statutes and judgments as righteous as this whole law which I am setting before you today? (Deut 4:6-8).

The parallels continue, consider these two verses, the first one from the New Testament:

But you are a chosen people, a royal priesthood, a holy nation, God's special possession, that you may declare the praises of him who called you out of darkness into his wonderful light (1 Pet 2:9).

This next verse is nearly identical, but this is from the Old Testament:

"Now if you obey me fully and keep my covenant, then out of all nations you will be my treasured possession. Although the whole earth is mine, you will be for me a kingdom of priests and a holy nation." These are the words you are to speak to the Israelites (Exod 19:5).

The world is craving a genuine representation of Jesus. Our lives and interactions with one another ought to be a picture of who He is to the world. We are priests representing God. Living in His abiding presence is supposed to let the world know we are disciples of Jesus. Jesus gave us a new command to love one another. The world really does want to know Him and He tells us that when we follow the command to love, they will.

THE COVENANT AND THE COMMAND

The establishment of the New Covenant can be found in Matthew 26:26-27, Mark 14:24, and Luke 22:20.

> And in the same way He took the cup after they had eaten, saying, "This cup which is poured out for you is the new covenant in My blood (Luke 22:20).

> A new commandment I give to you, that you love one another, even as I have loved you, that you also love one another. By this all men will know that you are My disciples, if you have love for one another (John 13:34-35).

You have read John 13–16 before, just as I have. The thing I never really understood was how critical this text is. Woven in between conversation and narrative, beautiful in its simplicity, we finally have a message about what people of faith had been waiting for: The New Covenant. Without pomp, fear and trembling, earthquakes, clouds and thick darkness over thundering mountains, or any other supernatural event of nature, the New Covenant came. Oh, it was still the voice of God, but this time God was a Man. This time the voice that thundered was so subtle I have been missing it for decades. *Yes, as it turns out, one can open up the Bible and point to the New Covenant, the terms and conditions, rules and ordinances.* They are just so completely different from Sinai and so unrecognizable compared to Abraham cutting covenant, it is easy to miss. Nevertheless, the passion and drama of God initiating a covenant with humanity is there in all its glory, from the intimacy of a private dinner, to the betrayal by a loved one, to one of the swiftest trials and subsequent executions ever read about. Our Father has quite the flare for the dramatic.

The essence of the New Covenant is here:

> I am the true vine, and My Father is the vinedresser. Every branch in Me that does not bear fruit, He takes away; and every branch that bears fruit, He prunes it so that it may bear more fruit. You are already clean because of the word which I have spoken to you. Abide in Me, and I in you. As the branch cannot bear fruit of itself unless it abides in the vine, so neither can you unless you abide in Me.
>
> I am the vine, you are the branches; he who abides in Me and I in him, he bears much fruit, for apart from Me you can do nothing. If anyone does not abide in Me, he is thrown away as a branch and dries up; and they gather them, and cast them into the fire and they are burned. If you abide in Me, and My words abide in you, ask whatever you wish, and it will be done for you. My Father is glorified by this, that you bear much fruit, and so prove to be My disciples.
>
> Just as the Father has loved Me, I have also loved you; abide in My love. If you keep My commandments, you will abide in My love; just as I have kept My Father's commandments and abide in His love.
>
> These things I have spoken to you so that My joy may be in you, and that your joy may be made full.
>
> This is My commandment, that you love one another, just as I have loved you. Greater love has no one than this, that one lay down his life for his friends. You are My friends if you do what I command you. No longer do I call you slaves, for the slave does not know what his master is do-

ing; but I have called you friends, for all things that I have heard from My Father I have made known to you. You did not choose Me but I chose you, and appointed you that you would go and bear fruit, and that your fruit would remain, so that whatever you ask of the Father in My name He may give to you. This I command you, that you love one another (John 15:1-17).

Astonishingly simple! The New Covenant is: Love one another as Jesus has loved you, and abide in Him.

Where is the long list of commands? Where is the specified behavior? Where are the do's and don'ts? What does God want of me? How do I know what He wants me to do? How do I know what His will for my life is? Trust Him to be good to His word, He will write these things on your heart and mind. "I will put My laws into their minds, and I will write them on their hearts. And I will be their God, and they shall be My people" (Heb 8:10).

John 15 tells us to abide in Him and to love like Jesus, but the thing I have never realized is the commands to love and abide *actually replace* the Mosaic Covenant! The curses and blessings have been replaced with something so confounding to the natural man that a few Bible teachers of today outright reject it. "If you abide in Me, and My words abide in you, ask whatever you wish, and it will be done for you. My Father is glorified by this, that you bear much fruit, and so prove to be My disciples" (John 15:7-8). Instead of reinterpreting what He *really meant,* redefining "whatever," or inventing reasons not universally supported in the body of Christ (e.g., God doesn't do miracles anymore), let's try abiding and exercising our faith. Let's ask a good deal more before we decide to not give the Father glory or to withhold proof of our discipleship. Because the truth is, the kingdom is accessed by faith. And, "without faith it's impossible to please God ... and He rewards those who seek Him" (Heb 11:6).

WALKING IT OUT

Jesus gave the new commandment, "Love one another as I have loved you" (John 13:34). He did not love passively. He actively loved. Love is active. Love does something, but what does it do? Love looks like something, but what does love look like? Jesus loved every person who came to Him, whether in faith or curiosity. Intriguingly, He did not love every person in the same way. To some He said, "Come follow me" (Matt 19:21). Another person begged Him, "Take me with you!" To which Jesus responded, "Return to your house and describe what great things God has done for you" (Luke 8:38-39).[7] Sometimes what is loving for Mary is of no consequence for Miguel. To be sure, love does not look the same in every situation. To make matters worse, sometimes what seems loving is occasionally hurtful in the end. Do we have to love every person who comes across our path? If not, then who? If so, I am exhausted just thinking about it!

The absence of these answers in Scripture is the very thing that will set you free if you allow it. Their absence is the very reason why I cannot tell you exactly what the new law is. Nevertheless, you do know what the answers are.

The answers to these questions are found written on your heart.

But now we have been released from this aspect of the Torah ... so that we are serving in the new way provided by the Spirit and not in the old way of outwardly following the letter of the law (Rom 7:6 CJB).

---

[7] The addendum to the story is the man went and told of all that God had done for him. The first time Jesus was in that area, the only people He encountered were two demon-possessed men living in a cemetery and a few pig herders. It was one of the demon-possessed men that Jesus freed, who was told to "return to your house and tell." Because the man obeyed, the next time Jesus showed up in that area, multitudes came out to meet Him.

> He has even made us competent to be workers serving a New Covenant, the essence of which is not a written text but the Spirit. For the written text brings death, but the Spirit gives life (2 Cor 3:6 CJB).

The Mosaic Covenant had many laws. They were tangible, written down by Moses. You could open a scroll and read them. The finger of God wrote some in stone. They were obvious to all, and there was no question as to precisely what they were. The New Covenant is completely different; it is the spoken words of Jesus. It came with one command and one ordinance. All other laws are still being written by the finger of God. Amazingly, this time the template for the finger of God is your heart and mind. The codes of the new law are written by the Spirit in your heart and mind. It is extraordinary to realize, but it is true. Jeremiah prophesied the transition and Hebrews repeats it. "Not like the covenant which I made with their fathers ... I will put My laws into their minds, and I will write them on their hearts" (Heb 8:9-10; Jer 31:31-33). The difference for us is that Hebrews confirms the prophecy now has been fulfilled.

Jeremiah was *not* prophesying that the Ten Commandments would be supernaturally transferred from stone tablets to hearts of flesh. Part of the prophecy includes all people knowing Him: "And they shall not teach everyone his fellow citizen, and everyone his brother, saying, 'Know the Lord,' for all will know Me" (Jer 31:34; Heb 8:11). How do we come to know Him? By hearing, listening to, and following His voice. Jesus said,

> The one who enters by the gate is the shepherd of the sheep ... the sheep listen to his voice ... and his sheep follow him because they know his voice ... I am the good shepherd; I know my sheep and my sheep know me ... I have other sheep that are not of this sheep pen. I must bring them also. They too will listen to my voice, and there shall be one

flock and one shepherd ... My sheep listen to my voice; I know them, and they follow me" (John 10:2-14).

The more familiar you are with His voice, the more you know Him.

He is now as promised, known by us, speaking to each of us, not just kings, priests, prophets, or a special someone chosen once in a generation. Jesus said it was good for Him to leave so that the Spirit could come. The Holy Spirit makes the New Covenant complete. We could not live under the New Covenant without Him, since He is the one who lives in our hearts and writes His laws and commands upon it. He speaks to our heart: "He who has ears to hear, let him hear what the Spirit says" (Rev 2:7). He is our teacher; He guides us into all things. First John re-emphasizes the fact in a different way: "As for you, the anointing which you received from Him abides in you, and you have no need for anyone to teach you; but as His anointing teaches you about all things, and is true and is not a lie, and just as it has taught you, you abide in Him" (1 John 2:27).

Do you see the progression of prophecy fulfilled? Jeremiah prophesied the New Covenant. He said under it we would know God, and God would write His laws on our heart. Jesus established the New Covenant. When He left He sent the Holy Spirit to be with us forever. The Holy Spirit now lives in our hearts and teaches us by writing His law on our hearts. We listen to and know His voice. Now that He is in us, it is possible to genuinely know God, just as Jeremiah said we would.

So let us get practical.

Someone may ask, "Okay, if I don't have to follow the law, then do I have to honor my mother and father?" My response would be, "What is the Holy Spirit asking you to do?" Are you asking the question because you do not want to honor your parents? If so, the answer is, "What does loving one another look like?" On the other hand, are you genuinely asking because

God is speaking to your heart? Has God put a radical call in your heart, yet your own fear or the council of others has you confused?

Because, let us be honest, someone seeking direction could open the Bible and read either:

> If anyone comes to Me, and does not hate his own father and mother and wife and children and brothers and sisters, yes, and even his own life, he cannot be My disciple (Luke 14:26).

Or they could read:

> But if anyone does not provide for his own, and especially for those of his household, he has denied the faith and is worse than an unbeliever (1 Tim 5:8).

We have seen the scenario before. If the above dilemma were to be presented to a learned person, a Doctor of Theology, or a long-time pastor, often the response would be to tear apart Scripture, look into the Greek text, the verb tenses, and try to reconcile the two verses. They would do that, because that is who they are. They are teachers; they love to learn and teach what they have learned. Even if the conflict gets intellectually satisfied, there can still be the internal unsettledness of the believer; we've all been through it. In those times the Spirit is on the move. Seek after Him. He has something to teach you. Pursue Him — He has treasures waiting and they are more than worth the wrestle. If the question of honoring one's parents were put to a fellow Christian, the answer given would be equal to the maturity of the spirit within that believer. Nevertheless, nobody can tell you what God is speaking to *your* heart, neither a theologian, nor a teacher, nor brother or sister in Jesus.

Only *you* know that.

Curiously, sometimes what is prudent (even your own wisdom) can get in the way of what the Spirit is trying to do in you by building your faith. Looking to the Bible for direction, without the guidance of the Holy Spirit, a person could get thoroughly confused. For example, though Jesus' first miracle involved making many gallons of wine, the book of Proverbs says that wine is a mocker. Furthermore, while Timothy was instructed to drink a little wine of his health, John made a vow that no fruit of the vine would touch his lips.

To settle the tension of both truths we need the Holy Spirit. With the Holy Spirit the newly-converted alcoholic's eyes are opened to the truth of his or her lifestyle. While in another circumstance the person under legalism is set free. The Holy Spirit leads us into all truth, our truth. He speaks to your heart; listen to Him.

In any scenario, if you ask 15 different people you will get 15 different answers. Nevertheless, the Spirit's answer on your heart will remain steady and constant. The unease from our human perspective comes because He is trying to build our faith. He most often does not answer our questions "how" or "why." There will simply remain the steady, "Yes, do," "No, don't," or some other annoyingly simple answer. The answer gives us just enough to take the next step, but never enough to see the whole picture.

INDIVIDUAL, NOT CORPORATE

The Old Covenant has precise guidelines within which one was to conduct life, from not worshiping other gods, to honest scales and tithing. Conquered Israel was displaced into Babylon. Why? Because they broke the covenant that said to "Have no other God's before Me" (Exod 20:3). The covenant said, if they worshiped other gods, they would serve another nation (Deut 28:32, 36). He was not *punishing* them for following other gods. They had *agreed* to be taken into bondage if they followed after other gods. Because our God cannot be found to be a liar, they were taken captive. Even so, it was after many generations of idol worship and Him pleading with them to turn back to Him. For it was His desire that, "the wicked man turns from all his sins which he has committed and observes all My statutes and practices justice and righteousness, he shall surely live" (Ezek 18:21-23). The Father did not *desire* Babylonian captivity, He desired a people to hold on to the One who loved them with an everlasting love. Sadly, they would not.

Under the Old Covenant, curses extended to the many because of the sins of a few. A singular example among many is in 2 Samuel 24. It records the story of David taking a census of the people. David acknowledged this act as sin, but the curse still came to the nation. David's numbering of the people caused 70,000 men in Israel to be killed.

This is good news for those under the New Covenant. We do not have to suffer the guilt and punishment of another man's sin. There was a parable in the ancient land of Israel "The fathers have eaten the sour grapes and the children's teeth are set on edge" (Jer 31:29). This was said because the children, or subsequent generations, suffered due to the actions of their fathers. Perhaps this is why the old rules and ordinances contain an admonishment to remove, sometimes by death (Lev 20:16; 24:16; Exod 21:15-17 to name a few), the law breaker. It was a protective measure on behalf of the community.

The good news is God promised a day when the descendants would not be punished for the sins of the fathers. Jeremiah declared, "In those days they will not say again, "The fathers have eaten sour grapes, and the children's teeth are set on edge." But everyone will die for his own iniquity; each man who eats the sour grapes, his teeth will be set on edge" (Jer 31:29). In Jeremiah's very next breath, he announced the news that would change everything. "Behold, days are coming," declares the Lord, "when I will make a new covenant" (Jer 31:30).

It is no longer a set of unwavering rules. You are not going to be cursed for someone else's sin. He knows where you've been, what you have been through, and what has been said to you. You are unique. There is no such thing as a one-size-fits-all believer's instruction manual. God knows you individually, and He alone knows what He is speaking to your heart. The fact is the whole New Covenant is all about freedom. It is all about: What is the Holy Spirit telling you? What is God speaking to your mind, writing on your heart? What is He asking *you?*

One eats meat sacrificed to idols, and one eats only vegetables, one regards a day as holy one does not. "Each must be fully convinced in his own mind" (Rom 14:5). Romans 14 is all about Paul explaining the very truth I am trying to reiterate. He says that he is convinced that nothing is clean or unclean, but if you deem it unclean, then for *you* it is! It has become a law for *you* but not necessarily for *others.* "The faith which you have, have as your own conviction before God" (Rom 14:22). Is this really true? My eating meat, or drinking wine, or whatever I do is a law for me? I can be convicted of something and others may not feel the same conviction?

Yes, it is true. Nevertheless, it is embedded in the command that we love one another. My paraphrase for the chapter is; "eat or drink whatever you'd like, as long as your conscience allows, but the moment you do harm to your brother, you are no longer acting in love and have broken the law of love." Without love, your conviction can be someone else's stumbling block. Paul goes to great lengths to address this very issue in Romans 14 and the first part of chapter 15. The following is a short excerpt:

But you, why do you judge your brother? Or you again, why do you regard your brother with contempt? For we will all stand before the judgment seat of God. For it is written, "As I live, says the Lord, every knee shall bow to me, and every tongue shall give praise to God." So then each one of us will give an account of himself to God. Therefore let us not judge one another anymore, but rather determine this—not to put an obstacle or a stumbling block in a brother's way. I know and am convinced in the Lord Jesus that nothing is unclean in itself; but to him who thinks anything to be unclean, to him it is unclean (Rom 14:10-14).

All of Romans 14:1–15:7 is a beautiful argument in favor of the rule of the Spirit of God in each of our unique hearts and minds, as opposed to the law on tablets of stone.

A word of caution: one must be careful to not require others to live according to the law in one's own heart. That is an open door for judgment and legalism. It is easy to be passionate about the things God is speaking to us, and understandable that we would want others to be as passionate as we are. It can also be frustrating to an impassioned person when others are not as equally moved. When God asks you to do something, more often than not, He is asking *you* to do it. He is usually not asking you to become a cheerleader to motivate others. Be convinced for yourself, but do not burden others with your conviction, nor judge them when they don't share your same convictions.

BUT, BUT, BUT

Even now, some may still be unwilling to let go of long-familiar teachings. They may think, "The law isn't all bad. What about murder? Are you saying I can now murder because I don't have to follow the law?" The Old Covenant and the new law of the Spirit are written by the same Deity, so of course there is going to be some overlap! *Love one another as I have loved you.* In what way could you conclude that murder would be loving someone in the same way Jesus loved? What about lying? Can we lie now that we are under the New Covenant? If you find yourself in a scenario in which it is more *loving* to lie than to tell the truth, then yes, you can lie.

Corrie Ten Boom lied to her neighbors when she said she was not housing Jews- but that is an extraordinary circumstance. How about, "Tell Grandma you love the thoughtful gift?" Is that a lie? Is it loving? Listen to the counsel of the Spirit.

This situation of the "thoughtful" gift from Grandma was a reality in our home one Christmas. My mother has always been attracted to dolls and has a small collection of unusual dolls. One year when my daughter was about six, my mother stumbled across some dolls that had "real expressions." They looked like middle-aged farmhands howling in agony, to be honest. Nevertheless, my mother found them completely delightful. My daughter did as she was told, which was to tell Grandma thank you and that she appreciated them. For months afterward, she was wracked with guilt knowing that she had lied to her grandmother. The law of "lying is a sin" had become completely oppressive to her. The law of love had not yet been discovered for our household.

We have learned much since that time. It can be tricky learning to navigate within the tension of abiding in Him without a written code and yet within the confines of loving God and one another. The initial steps are uncertain and shaky, but you will gain certain confidence in His leading in a very short while.

I had a brief encounter with a woman who was caring for her elderly father afflicted with Alzheimer's disease. As a Christian, she believed lying was sin. Sadly, there were times during his care that the truth caused him frustration and agitation. In order to ease his agitation, she would occasionally lie to him. The lying induced guilt in her, even when she knew it was more loving to her ailing father to tell the lie. Eventually her father died, but the feelings of guilt remained. It was not until she learned the law of the Spirit, the law of love that she finally felt released and found freedom from the guilt. Her relief was quite apparent at discovering the heart of her heavenly Father toward her predicament.

I once read an article from a church that borrowed money to build an additional campus for their ministry. The article explained how they had concluded it was not detrimental to their ministry to borrow money. Instead of starting out with what God was saying to this particular fellowship, George Mueller's life convictions were examined.

Mueller is a personal hero of mine. He was absolutely convinced that he was not to ask people for help with his ministry needs. He was to be dependent on God to provide. Mueller took all of his needs to God in prayer, and God provided. His story is quite inspirational. Surprisingly, this other ministry looked at Mueller and his Scriptural convictions to "owe no man anything" and concluded he was wrong in his convictions! He was not wrong. Mueller heard from God regarding the ministry entrusted to him. God had given instruction to Mueller, and he lived by the faith and conviction that God had spoken to him. Furthermore, he did not require that others live by his convictions. This other ministry, which dismantled Mueller's position on borrowing, came to their own different conclusions for the purchase of their property.

God speaks to each of us and writes His laws on our individual hearts. What He is asking of one ministry is not necessarily what God is asking of another ministry. Ideally, all are serving God according to where they believe God is giving direction. It is really unnecessary to invalidate someone's position in order to validate the faith-walk God has laid before you.

Why does one ministry have to be wrong in order for another to walk confidently in the Lord's leading down a different path? It would be so much better if we encouraged one another to seek what the Spirit is saying. If one has a word from the Lord, and he is fully convinced in his own mind, he is walking in faith. "The faith you have, have as your own conviction before God" (Rom 14:22).

It should not matter if someone has come to a different conviction than you. If you have asked God, sought Scripture, prayed, and received a word, then trust the Spirit to lead you. Godly counsel from men is advisable, of course, but man's opinion should not be the final authority. Be open to the Spirit completely changing your perspective, because God alone is able to know all the unseen variables. If you are seeking Him, trust Him to guide you into all truth. Believe that He is able to keep you. If He is able to save you, He is more than able to keep you. If you start to choose wrongly, trust that He will speak to you. If you keep yourself open to correction, you need not be immobilized by fear of doing the wrong thing. Get moving, get doing, but always be mindful of the Spirit within. It is called "abiding," the thing we are supposed to be doing every day anyhow. If He gives instruction, follow it. If He does not give instruction, proceed in your choice until He tells you otherwise. Trust the Spirit in you to counsel you. He is the Wonderful Counselor, it is what He does. Of course there is the confirmation of the Spirit within the body of believers, and it is always wise to seek out prayer and wisdom from the saints. That being said, I think that the Body has been top heavy in that direction. The ministry of the Spirit within the individual has been marginalized to the point of neglect in some circles.

I realize this is a new concept for many. Undoubtedly, you will find freedom if you choose to pursue the law of the Spirit. The Spirit frees you from the all the "shoulds" of the Christian "religion." I love reading the Bible and do so as often as I am able. The Bible has stories of people who studied the Scripture and knew it well; Jesus quoted it all the time. Paul "reasoned from the scriptures" (Acts 17:2) constantly. The men of Berea are always an honorable example (Acts 17:11). Apollos is another example (Acts 18:24). Yet, where is it written we should read the Bible daily? Condemnation comes quickly on the heels of "clever" sayings like, "Seven days without reading your Bible makes one weak." During the first couple of centuries, Christians got along famously without the Book. Nobody could ever accuse them of being weak. Almost no one had a Bible until Gutenberg's printing press came along in 1450, and even then, only the most wealthy had them. Maybe it really is Who you know, not what you know, that makes all the difference.

I am not saying we should not read our Bibles. Of course we should read our Bibles! Do it, because it is wonderful! Read it often, without believing the lie that when you don't, you have somehow failed. The truth is we should do many things. In fact we "should" do so many different and varied things that it is impossible to do them all. The question is no longer, "What should I do?" There are a thousand answers to that. Rather the question ought to be, "God, what is on Your heart? What do You want me to do in this situation?" When you know what God is asking of you by faith, guilt, manipulation, or the fear of man become utterly powerless.

A friend attended a church in which it was often preached that a believer should rise up early and have a quiet time to pray and read. She went around with this for years. She is not wired that way. Her quiet time was at night, when no looming schedule of school or work was beckoning. Her head is clear and awareness keen in the evening. Though she spent hours in the evening reading and studying her Bible, she felt guilty for not being obedient and doing the "right thing." The right thing is that we seek God. Period. In retrospect of that time, she decided it was the rules of man being imposed on her, not the call of the Spirit. Why did she come to that conclusion? There were a few reasons. It eventually became clear that following the rule of waking up early became the primary focus. The constant feeling of guilt began fading in direct correlation to the growing conviction that she was loved with an everlasting love. One day the truth of freedom fully dawned on her; she was pursuing Jesus and a relationship with Him because she loved Him. She now knows the time of the day spent communing with Him does not determine her depth of love for Him.

... LET HIM HEAR WHAT THE SPIRIT SAYS

Let us look at a biblical model of something so out of reach of our understanding, were it to happen today, it would likely cause the greatest church split in history. It stands solidly as a stellar example of exactly what happens when the Holy Spirit speaks to those who have ears to hear what the Spirit is saying. In Acts 15, at the Council of Jerusalem, it was decided that Gentile believers in the Jewish Messiah did not have to follow the laws of Moses. Neither did they have to be circumcised to be included in the Abrahamic Covenant (Circumcision came over 400 years before The Law was written, going back to Abraham). What text was consulted? What Scripture was quoted? How did they come to a monumental decision like that? In fact, the weight of that decision cannot be accurately weighed in the course of human events, the repercussions extending too far, too deep into the last 2,000 years of history.

The belief that circumcision was required for new believers had been introduced to the Church. To settle the matter, a meeting was arranged with Paul and Barnabas, the Apostles and the elders. There was much discussion, and some believers who were of the sect of the Pharisees said the Gentiles must be circumcised. It is nothing less than shocking to realize the Pharisees were absolutely correct in their literal interpretation of the written word when they said, "It is necessary to circumcise [the Gentiles]" (Acts 15:5). For the Pharisees knew *it stands written in the Holy Scriptures*:

> Every male among you who is eight days old shall be circumcised throughout your generations, a servant who is born in the house or who is bought with money from any foreigner, who is not of your descendants. A servant who is born in your house or who is bought with your money shall surely be circumcised; thus shall My covenant be in your flesh for an everlasting covenant. But an uncircumcised male who is not circumcised in the flesh of his foreskin, that person shall be cut off from his people; he has broken My covenant (Gen 17:12-14).

So the sect of the Pharisees reasoned according to Scripture that if the Gentiles were to be included with father Abraham, they must be circumcised. The stunning realization here is *the Pharisees had a solid Scripture to back up their position!*

Are you letting that sink in?

It actually sounds like a really good argument to me. If I were there, I know it's likely I would have been swayed to believe Gentiles ought to be circumcised. I think many people would have sided with what has been written. But, the Holy Spirit had been invited to the meeting, and He wasn't swayed by the written Word. He saw things differently.

I cannot say it enough. We have a New Covenant where the Spirit writes His laws in our heart and mind. The Apostles gave attention to what the Holy Spirit was saying. They chased the wind of the Spirit not knowing where He was going and found that He was saying a new thing (John 3:8).

Astonishingly, *no* Scripture was quoted as foundational for what happened next. The Spirit wrote a brand new law on the hearts and minds of those gathered. No, the Gentiles did not have to be circumcised. Most remarkably, the decision that changed the course of Christianity from a Jewish sect into a completely new religion was based on: "It seemed good to the Holy Spirit and to us" (Acts 15:28). They saw God moving in signs wonders and miracles in the lives of the Gentiles. Based on the observations of what God was doing on the outside and discerning what the Holy Spirit was writing on the inside, they made a decision that forever changed the course of history.

"He who has an ear, let him hear what the Spirit says to the churches" (Rev 2:7).[8] Has He been laying something on your heart? Trust Him to lead you where you need to go. If He is able to draw you to Him in the first place, He is more than able to keep you with Him always.

NEW COVENANT MORE DEMANDING THAN THE OLD COVENANT?

It has been suggested that the New Covenant is more demanding and more difficult to keep than the Old. Like the answer to the question, "Can I do whatever I want?" the response is both yes and no. Much of it depends on your level of abiding. It has been said living under Grace requires more from me than the Old Covenant, because under the old, I simply could not commit adultery. Under the New, lusting is equated to committing adultery. Under the Old, you could not murder, while under grace, hating is as murder.

Grace is not the replacement of the Old Covenant. In a nutshell, Jesus is the replacement of the Old Covenant. "For the Law was given through Moses; grace and truth were realized through Jesus Christ" (John 1:17). Grace is great favor. Under Law the servants of God were ruled by a system of justice and punishment, action and reaction. In Jesus, the former "serv-

---

[8] The instruction to hear what the Spirit says is given seven times in Revelation 2–3, and Jesus repeated it constantly in His ministry.

ants" have found great favor. We have gone from slave to friend to son (John 15:15). We are now sons and daughters of the Living God, called, chosen, blessed, beloved, adopted, redeemed, and forgiven (Ephesians 1). We have been included in His will and been given an inheritance.

Even so, I have heard it taught that living in grace is more difficult and requires more than the law. This is out of the frying pan and into the fire. Believing that favor (for that is what grace is) demands more than the law does not understand the heart of grace. Neither does grace *demand,* nor does it *require,* because that would not be great favor. The assertion does not hold up to the scrutiny of Scripture. Do you remember the council at Jerusalem, where it was decided that the Gentiles do not have to follow the Laws of Moses? Recall what Peter said:

> And God, who knows the heart, testified to them giving them the Holy Spirit, just as He also did to us; and He made no distinction between us and them, cleansing their hearts by faith. Now therefore why do you put God to the test by placing upon the neck of the disciples a yoke which neither our fathers nor we have been able to bear? But we believe that we are saved through the grace of the Lord Jesus, in the same way as they also are (Acts 15:8-11).

Peter did not think that living in grace required more than the Law of Moses. If the yoke of Moses were unbearable, and nobody could keep it, how could we be expected to do *more* than the law? What a burden to bear! What a relief for all believers. Peter understood that faith is the only requirement for grace. Peter knew that grace stands in direct contrast to laws and ordinances; though it is not a replacement, it is everything they are not. His speech that day confidently asserts that belief. Grace is a *gift* (Rom 5:15; Eph 3:7); it is not a heavier burden than the law.

The truth of the matter is, typically the only time in which I hear grace requires more than the law is when preachers are asking for an offering. Most often grace is taught as a gift freely given that covers over all sins. Except for when tithes and offerings are being collected, then in the context of giving we are asked to go beyond the law. *"We are not under the ten percent law. No, we are under grace, and grace requires more than the law. Grace requires our all,"* says the person receiving the offering. In the offering there is but one law, the law of the harvest. "Now this I say, he who sows sparingly will also reap sparingly, and he who sows bountifully will also reap bountifully. Each one must do just as he has purposed in his heart, not grudgingly or under compulsion, for God loves a cheerful giver" (2 Cor 9:6-7). Sometimes sowing bountifully can be a stretch at twenty dollars; other times 2,000 dollars would be giving sparingly.

Paradoxically at times, those who believe grace requires more in the offering, will apply it differently when someone sins and feels great condemnation. Grace now rightly applied, is the balm that soothes the soul. It reaches out to comfort a hurting brother or sister. Grace is a gift of God freely given, washing you clean and making you righteous. Grace is all this and more; it gives us power, not just pardon.

We are indeed under grace, grace and truth through Jesus. Grace, a gift of favor freely given is in no way more burdensome than the law. The law was a burden which neither the Apostles nor their fathers were able to bear. We have a better, more superior covenant. The New Covenant is love.

Yet, love can be quite difficult. It asks us to do things that we sometimes would rather not. To love takes an active choice, and that choice does not always come easily. Sometimes choosing to love is one of the most difficult things the Spirit can ask of us.

So, what about the "hate is murder," "lust is adultery" teaching of Jesus? I believe that Jesus was addressing the hearts of those in His hearing. God is after our hearts. The Spirit of God makes known to us the thoughts and attitudes of the heart (Heb 4:12-13). The purpose is that we repent of them and be made right to love. Lusting after another is not loving. It reduces the person to slave status, because it makes the person lusted after into an object to fulfill one's desire. Lust does not take into account the fallout and repercussions of all who would be affected if it were satisfied. Under the law, you technically could get away with murder provided you planned it well and fled to a sanctuary city (Num 35:25). Hate is a continuous condition of one's heart. Love is considerate of all. Law judges behaviors but Love looks at the heart. "For God sees not as man sees, for man looks at the outward appearance, but the LORD looks at the heart" (1 Sam 16:7).

The abiding Spirit who asks me to love can make all kinds of requests of me, I have said yes to the covenant. However, I can make no demands for reciprocal love. Should I demand that someone love me, I am no longer acting in love. The truth that love can make no demands is foremost to understanding the type of fellowship (i.e. church gathering) to which you willingly submit yourself. All service within the context of church ought to be a freewill offering of love toward others. Your service should never be required or coerced through guilt. If you find yourself within an authoritarian-style fellowship that demands rather than requests, I would suggest you seek confirmation of the Spirit on continued attendance.

So yes, the New Covenant is more difficult, because God addresses our hearts and attitudes. It is a whole lot easier to give a fellow a denarius at the temple than it is to invite him into your home and cook him a meal. Yet, that may be what the Spirit is asking of you.

On the other hand, abiding with the Spirit can free you from the should-have's and ought-to's of being a "good Christian." As you become increasingly aware of the abiding presence of the Spirit, things get simplified. You do not have to wonder if you should, or feel guilty you didn't. When you are abiding in Him, you know what to do. Personally and surprisingly, I have discovered that He requests a lot less than man, and even my own self expectations. The Holy Spirit is not a Pharisee who "[Ties] up heavy, cumbersome loads and [puts] them on other people's shoulders, but they themselves are not willing to lift a finger to move them" (Matt 23:4).

To the contrary, Jesus' yoke is light.

> *Come to me, all you who are weary and burdened, and I will give you rest. Take my yoke upon you and learn from me, for I am gentle and humble in heart, and you will find rest for your souls. For My yoke is easy and My burden is light (Matt 11:28-30).*

4

CAN YOU TRUST YOUR HEART?

The heart is more deceitful than all else
And is desperately sick;
Who can understand it?
Jeremiah 17:9

With an overemphasis on the Jeremiah 17:9, there has been a teaching in the church, which says we cannot trust our hearts. Many of us have been told our mind is the master and tells us the truth of the Word. "Trust your mind it knows the truth, you can't trust your feelings or your heart," goes the advice. "We bind the Law on our mind!"

Using Matthew 22:37 (Love the Lord your God with all your heart, with all your soul, and with all your mind), some pastors emphasize the *mind* as the primary importance virtually ignoring the heart and soul. Having correct doctrine is the high-water mark for some who study the Scriptures. But Jesus said the reason to study the Scriptures is because they tell of Him (John 5:39). The study of Scripture ought to bring you closer to the Living God. They are to provide the backdrop and context for the voice that now speaks to your heart, not give you a better argument than the next guy. I am in no way advocating the disregard of Scripture and doctrine; rather, also encouraging daily communing with the Spirit. There is a strong emphasis within the church on knowing and meditating on the Word. Encouragement is often given that Scripture should be memorized in order to be "hidden in our heart." After all, "Thy word have I hidden in my heart that I might not sin against thee" (Ps 119:11). There seems to be fear in the occasional leader who thinks if people follow their hearts, they will, like sheep or lemmings, run headlong into folly and deception. The fear underscores the sad truth that these leaders have little faith in the power of the Holy Spirit to keep us. Scripture memorization has merit, but the Holy Spirit is perfect at bringing Scripture to mind when needed. We should be mindful that *Jesus* is the Word of God hidden in our hearts. It is He who is to be hidden in our heart. It is He, by His Holy Spirit instructing our hearts and speaking to them. The Bible is scripture, and Scripture teaches undeniably that Jesus is the Word of God (John 1:14). When you listen to your heart, listen for His voice. If you aren't sure how, or what His voice sounds like, help will be offered in a later chapter: *What Does the Holy Spirit Sound Like?*

YES, YOU CAN TRUST YOUR HEART!

Be encouraged, if you have the Holy Spirit, you absolutely can trust your heart. The truth is, Scripture after Scripture says that the wise man has a good heart. We know the wise man trusts the Lord with his whole heart. Jesus said the hearts of men *can* be bad, but He also said men's hearts *can be good*:

The good man brings good things out of the good stored up in his heart, and the evil man brings evil things out of the evil stored up in his heart. For out of the overflow of his heart his mouth speaks (Luke 6:45).

But the seed on good soil stands for those with a noble and good heart, who hear the word, retain it, and by persevering produce a crop (Luke 8:15).

Blessed are the pure in heart, for they will see God (Matt 5:8).

For where your treasure is, there your heart will be also (Matt 6:21).

Jesus replied: "Love the Lord your God with all your heart and with all your soul and with all your mind" (Matt 22:37).

A deceitful, desperately sick heart could not love God, let alone be the place Jesus lives. The acknowledgement that people do have good hearts, hearts that seek the Lord, is not just in the New Testament.

The Lord looks at the heart (2 Sam 17:11).

For the eyes of the Lord move to and fro throughout the earth that He may strongly support those whose heart is completely His (2 Chr 16:9).

But from there you will seek the LORD your God, and you will find Him if you search for Him with all your heart and all your soul (Deut 4:29).

Watch over your heart with all diligence, for from it flow the springs of life (Prov 4:23).

Consider the story of Abimelech, a pagan king who took Abraham's wife, Sarah, to be his wife. God Himself testified that Abimelech's heart was one of integrity. Here is the conversation between Abimelech and God:

> Did he not himself say to me, "She is my sister"? And she herself said, "He is my brother." In the integrity of my heart and the innocence of my hands I have done this." Then God said to him in the dream, "Yes, I know that in the integrity of your heart you have done this, and I also kept you from sinning against Me" (Gen 20:5-6).

David, called "a man after God's heart" (Acts 13:22) wrote a song with lyrics that are still sung 3,000 years later. "Create in me a clean heart, O God, and renew a steadfast spirit within me" (Ps 51:10).

Any Bible scholar will tell you the word "create" used in this Psalm means to create a brand new thing from new material. God does not re-work the old heart of sin into a clean heart; He creates a brand new, clean heart. He creates one that is pure, a heart that is good; it is a temple the Holy Spirit lives in and sends forth His decrees. You have to ignore a lot of Scripture which pointedly says otherwise to conclude that, above all else, a man's heart is only deceitful and desperately sick all the time.

CONTEXT, CONTEXT

In all honesty, the verse about the heart being deceitful above all else cannot simply be ignored. All Scripture is God-breathed and useful for teaching. Since one of the rules for Bible interpretation is "context is king," let us look at the context for this passage. When read contextually, we see it is God's assessment of the heart of Judah. This nation followed generations of evil and wicked kings and had gone from displeasing to defiled. For generations they worshiped false gods, sacrificed their children in the fire, committed spiritual adultery, and constantly turned away from the statutes and laws of God. Because of this, God called Jeremiah to plead the case of the LORD to the nation. Jeremiah wept over the hard hearts that refused to turn back to God and be healed. Rather than repentance, they chose Babylonian subjugation. The verse of the heart being desperately wicked is often quoted to give evidence that the heart of all of humanity is evil. Yet looking at the verse in context there is no way you can conclude that God was saying all men, everywhere, through all generations, have wicked hearts.

> Blessed is the man who trusts in the LORD
> And whose trust is the LORD.
> For he will be like a tree planted by the water,
> That extends its roots by a stream
> And will not fear when the heat comes;
> But its leaves will be green,
> And it will not be anxious in a year of drought
> Nor cease to yield fruit.
> The heart is more deceitful than all else
> And is desperately sick;
> Who can understand it?
> I, the LORD, search the heart,
> I test the mind,
> Even to give to each man according to his ways,
> According to the results of his deeds (Jer 17:7-10).

Yes, hearts that are void of the Spirit can be deceitful and wicked, but they are not when the Holy Spirit lives in and has rulership over that heart. We read, "But the one who joins himself to the Lord is one spirit with Him" (1 Cor 6:17). We pray for God to come into our heart and live within it. We ask Him to take up residence and reign there. Then we are told that we cannot trust the voice that speaks from there. We learn to hush the voice from well-meaning people who have themselves been taught the heart is deceitful and wicked. This idea of a deceitful heart has been around since the Middle Ages. Truthfully, it has no basis in the teachings of Jesus or the rest of Scripture in regards to a person who has a renewed heart.

LISTEN TO YOUR HEART

Not surprisingly, after being taught they cannot trust their hearts, people can end up believing, "God just doesn't talk to me in that way." This is because the heart is the place from which the Spirit speaks. They have trained their brains to listen to logic and common sense over the voice of the Spirit (which is often wild, untamed and, even illogical). What kind of battle plan is it to march in silence for seven days around a city (Josh 6:2-5)? What logic is there in sending out worshipers in front of an army (2 Chr 20:14-23)? Does anyone understand the reasoning behind the gift of tongues? It is especially illogical when the people who hear it are likely to think you are either drunk or crazy (Act 2:13; 1 Cor 14:23)!

Read any modern day biography of anyone who did great things for God—William Carey, Reese Howells, Jim Elliot, Gladys Allward, Amy Carmichael, just to name a brief few. They all followed the voice in their heart over and above the advice of concerned contemporaries, even those who were older in the Lord, good common sense and the dictates of logic. Even so, they are all held in high regard as people who knew God and did great things for Him. Not one of them is exemplified for excellent doctrine. They may have had great doctrine, but when their stories are told, the focus is their faith and devotion to Jesus. Most consistently, the Spirit gives no good reason for the leading in your heart. If He did, it would not be walking by faith. God does not give you a blueprint of your life and answer all of the what-if's. He is the Lord, and your job is to follow the instruction, not to understand it. To understand something helps us to feel in control of our lives, almost everyone is far more comfortable when they feel they have a certain amount of control over their affairs. Understandably, that is why it is easy to allow logic and "good common sense" to override the wild notions of the heart.

It is possible you have trained your brain to hush the still small voice of the Spirit. The good news is He is still speaking to you. He never stopped. If you believe He does not speak, or you feel you have not heard Him in a while, you can retrain your spiritual ears. The fact is, you really cannot shut off the voice of your heart entirely. New scientific findings have discovered that the heart can and does think, and it has sway over your brain! This is phenomenal!

> Scientific evidence pointed out that, in fact, the heart can dictate the brain which is touted as a more rational and conventionally more pragmatic decision maker. According to the Institute of Heartmath, the heart communicates with the brain in ways that influence how we perceive and respond to stimulus coming from the outside world. The heart can even cause the brain to obey its commands. The heart has its own little brain as 40,000 neurons were found in it!

> This observation is further substantiated by anecdotal evidences in the medical field. These are at best anecdotal because heart transplants are not that commonly performed. And it would be unethical to experiment on people. Pending more rigorous scientific investigations, heart transplant cases appear to confirm the theory that the heart thinks in-

dependently. Amazingly, heart recipients exhibited their donor's lifestyle and way of thinking.[9]

Also:

> Groundbreaking research in the field of neurocardiology has established that the heart is a sensory organ and a sophisticated information encoding and processing center, with an extensive intrinsic nervous system sufficiently sophisticated to qualify as a "heart brain" ... Armour discusses intriguing data documenting the complex neuronal processing and memory capabilities of the intrinsic cardiac nervous system, indicating that the heart brain can process information and make decisions about its control independent of the central nervous system. By providing an understanding of the elaborate anatomy and physiology of the cardiac nervous system, this monograph contributes to the newly emerging view of the heart as a complex, self-organized system that maintains a continuous two-way dialogue with the brain and the rest of the body.[10]

Blaise Pascal, a scientist-turned-Christian philosopher, after a "second conversion" in the 17th century, said, "The heart has reasons that reason cannot know." He had no idea just how accurate he was. Four hundred years later, science has caught up with the truth that God had put on his heart.

---

[9] Patrick Regoniel, "Do You Know that the Heart Can Think?" http://scienceray.com/biology/human-biology/do-you-know-that-the-heart-can-think/ Last accessed January 15, 2014.

[10] More can be read in this 19 page eBook: Andrew Armour, "Neurocardiology—Anatomical and Functional Principles" http://www.heartmathstore.com/cgi-bin/category.cgi?item=enro&source=ihmsrc&kw=generallink. Last accessed January 15, 2014.

5

THE PASSOVER,
THE NEW COVENANT,
& THE KINGDOM

"What makes tonight different
from all other nights?"
"Once we were slaves and now we are free."
~ From the Passover Celebration

Jesus instituted the New Covenant on Passover. That fact alone ought to give us pause and make us want to look deeper into the significance of the two events coinciding. Above all else, Passover is a celebration of freedom; freedom from slavery for the Jew, and freedom from the old law for the followers of Jesus. "For the law of the Spirit of life in Christ Jesus has set you free from the law of sin and of death" (Rom 8:2).

He appeared after His resurrection and, "He said to them, 'These are My words which I spoke to you while I was still with you, that all things which are written about Me in the Law of Moses and the Prophets and the Psalms must be fulfilled'" (Luke 24:44). I cannot prove definitively which cups were drunk and celebrated at Passover or whether Jesus and His disciples drank four or five cups. He was fulfilling many things that night. Nevertheless, He said *all* must be fulfilled. "Fulfilled" is an aorist Greek verb, which means it is an action that *occurred in the past.* This past fulfillment includes Psalms 2.

> You are My Son, Today I have begotten You. Ask of Me, and I will surely give the nations as Your inheritance, And the very ends of the earth as Your possession (Ps 2:7-8).

On Passover God delivered the Jews out of slavery in Egypt and led them to a "fair and good land" (Deut 3:25). God had given the promise to Moses for the Israelites, "I will bring you to the land which I swore to give to Abraham, Isaac, and Jacob, and I will give it to you for a possession; I am the LORD" (Exod 6:8). Jesus said that all things written of Him must be fulfilled (a past tense fulfillment). On Passover, Jesus did it! He delivered us from the law of sin and death, into a good land. He has brought us into the land sworn to Abraham and "his Seed" (Rom 3:14). "If you belong to Christ, then you are Abraham's seed, and heirs according to the promise" (Gal 3:29). The nations are His inheritance, the whole earth His possession, and He has given it to us. As co-heirs it has become *our* inheritance as well.

Colossians tells us the Passover, along with other feasts and traditions, have as much ability to be comprehended as a shadow. Shadows do have some details, but for a full picture to be seen the shadow needs to be "fleshed out." This happens in Jesus. "Let no man therefore judge you in meat or drink, or in respect to a holy day or the new moon or the Sabbath days, which are a shadow of things to come, but the body is of Christ" (Col 2:16-17). The Passover is a holy day and as such, a prophetic shadow of Jesus. He fulfilled the promises in Exodus 6:8 "I will bring you to the land … I am the Lord." The long-anticipated Kingdom of the Messiah had come, not in the physical, but by the Spirit. Regardless, the Kingdom is real and we have been invited to enter in, a kingdom in which we rule alongside Him by faith.

> All authority has been given to Me in heaven and on earth. Go therefore and make disciples of all the nations, baptizing them in the name of the Father and the Son and the Holy Spirit, teaching them to observe all that I commanded you; and lo, I am with you always, even to the end of the age (Matt 28:18-20).

Upon resurrection, Jesus declared himself to be in authority over the whole earth. He then extended His authority to the apostles and those who would follow after.

AUTHORITY

We must pause here briefly to understand the word "authority" that Jesus used when He said, "All authority has been given to Me in heaven and on earth. Go ..." Authority is a common word and when words are familiar we read them without considering if there is a deeper meaning. In our day "authority" has lost some of the impact it used to carry. The Greek *exousia* which has been translated into authority means: "Power as entrusted, i.e., commission, authority, right, full power; Power over persons and things, dominion, authority, rule."[11] In English, "Authority" stems from the word *autor* (later changed to author, and then eventually expanded to authority). *Autor* meant: "father, master, leader, founder, enlarger, one who causes to grow."[12] When the Bible was translated from the Lat-

---

[11] Spiros Zodhiates, The Complete Word Study Dictionary: New Testament (Chattanooga, TN: AMG, 1993), 606.

[12] "Author." http://dictionary.reference.com/browse/author. Last accessed: January 18, 2014.

in manuscripts into English, Tyndale and men like him had the understanding that Jesus" declarative position over heaven and earth to be "Master." Mastery, leadership, full power, rulership, and dominion are His. Earth was no longer the possession of the enemy, earth was back in the hands of the leader and founder. The Author of Creation had finally and fully redeemed what was rightfully His. The Kingdom, His Inheritance was His to command. He then took His inheritance and authority and gave it to you, His Bride.

PICTURES WITHIN PICTURES

One of the fascinating things about Scripture is the multiple layers of prophecy. There are outright prophecies such as, "You will be the father of many nations" (Gen 17:4 NIV). This is a direct statement about the future. Another layer of prophecy is in the stories. The whole story of the Exodus and conquest of the Promised Land becomes a vaguely familiar prophetic picture telling of another freedom and Kingdom. The "second and final exodus" from slavery and into the Kingdom of God would have a leader who often ascended the mountain to talk with God face to face. He would also do signs and wonders among the people before the final conquest of the Promised Land. Moses said to look for "a prophet like me" (Deut 18:15). They were looking for someone to follow after the footsteps of Moses, but the reality is Moses was not the prototype. Jesus is the original and Moses gave us only glimpses of Jesus. Israel was set free from the bondage and slavery of Egypt, while those in the Kingdom know that physical freedom, which is of inestimable worth, is only just the beginning. Moses lead Israel to an abundant land filled with goodness, health, long life, prosperity, peace and wholeness. Alternately, Jesus led us to the Kingdom, complete with its promises, and willed all of it to us, thus fulfilling the prophetic shadows. Interestingly, the entrance and access to both Kingdoms, the land of Israel beyond the Jordan and the Kingdom of God, both hinge on just one thing: *Belief.*

Albeit aggressively confident belief: passive belief will not get you there. Israel did not passively gain their inheritance, and neither will you.

> Now it came about ... that the Lord spoke to Joshua ... saying, "Moses My servant is dead; now therefore arise ... you and all this people, to the land which I am giving to them ... Every place on which the sole of your foot treads, I have given it to you, just as I spoke to Moses ... No man will be able to stand before you all the days of your life ... I will not fail you or forsake you. Be strong and courageous, for you shall give this people possession of the land (Josh 1:1-6).

Jesus, like Joshua, is bringing us into our inheritance. Like the Israelites before us, so we too must *take* our inheritance by faith. Be strong and courageous, knowing God will not fail or forsake you. The promises waiting to be had in the Kingdom must be taken; they will not be handed to you. "Violent men take it by force" (Matt 11:6).

... WITHIN PICTURES

When God led the nation into Canaan to take as their possession, one of the things He promised was reprieve from the curse. No, the Scripture does not say those words exactly. When God cursed the ground on account of Adam, saying it would yield thorns and thistles, He promised otherwise to those who walked in His ways. God promised He would "husband" the land. Consider:

Therefore, you shall keep the commandments of the Lord your God, to walk in His ways and to fear Him. For the Lord your God is bringing you into a good land, a land of brooks of water, of fountains and springs, flowing forth in valleys and hills; a land of wheat and barley, of vines and fig trees and pomegranates, a land of olive oil and honey; a land where you will eat food without scarcity, in which you will not lack anything; a land whose stones are iron, and out of whose hills you can dig copper. When you have eaten and are satisfied, you shall bless the Lord your God for the good land which He has given you (Deut 8:6-10).

It is a land the LORD your God cares for; the eyes of the LORD your God are continually on it from the beginning of the year to its end (Deut 11:12).

Don't you just love the pictures He paints? Did you see it? Israel has long been called His Bride, His beloved. As Husband (Isa 54:5), He adores and cares for His Bride. He brought her into a land in which He would "husband" her. Though the ground was cursed because of Adam, this new land was to be a land that He cared for. All she had to do was be faithful to her Lover.

Nothing has changed.

We are the Bride of Christ, His chosen beloved. He adores and cares for you, you are the Beloved of the Lord. He brought us into the Kingdom, where He will "husband" us, care for us and He has forever dealt with the curse! When we abide in His Love we can ask whatever we wish, and it will be done.

THE CUP OF SUFFERING AND OF THE NEW COVENANT

Recall Hebrews once again "For where a covenant is, there must of necessity be the death of the one who made it … Therefore even the first covenant was not inaugurated without blood" (Heb 9:16,18). Jesus compared His crucifixion and suffering to drinking a cup. He made reference to this when James and John asked if they could sit on His right and left hand in His kingdom. His response was, "You don't know what you are asking … can you drink the cup I am going to drink?" (Matt 20:22). At least three times Jesus referred to his crucifixion as a "cup of suffering" (Matt 20:22-23; Matt 26:39; John 18:11).[13] Coinciding with calling the crucifixion a cup, He also called one of the cups served at the Passover meal the "cup of the New Covenant in [His] blood" (the blood of course corresponds to the crucifixion). The crucifixion, His blood, the New Covenant, Passover and the Kingdom cannot be viewed separately.

At one point during the Passover meal, "He had taken a cup and given thanks, He said, "Take this and share it among yourselves; for I say to you, I will not drink of the fruit of the vine from now on until the kingdom of God comes"" (Luke 22:17-18). Later when supper was ended, He addressed the last cup of the meal. Seemingly, He did not drink that one. He said, "This cup which is poured out for you," implying He did not drink it but poured it out (for though it was close the Kingdom had not yet come). "This cup which is poured out for you is the new covenant in My blood" (Luke 22:20). The cup was indeed the New Covenant in His blood, but He did not drink the cup just

---

[13] Jesus was not the first to use this cup-as-suffering metaphor; it was used often in the Old Testament. For instance, the Book of Job says, "Let their own eyes see their destruction; let them drink the cup of the wrath of the Almighty" (Job 21:20).

then. But one could probably feel the weight of the Kingdom pressing in.

The book of Matthew records that Jesus was offered wine twice while He was being crucified. The first time was a little early on. "They gave Him wine to drink mixed with gall; and after tasting it, He was unwilling to drink it" (Matt 27:34). Later on, Matthew records: "Immediately one of them ran, and taking a sponge, he filled it with sour wine and put it on a reed, and gave Him a drink. But the rest of them said, "Let us see whether Elijah will come to save Him." And Jesus cried out again with a loud voice, and yielded up His spirit" (Matt 27:48-50). All was fulfilled He drank the last cup of Passover, His crucifixion, and simultaneously the fruit of the vine. *His Kingdom had fully come*!

In His last passionate breath He declared victory to His Bride (Rev 19:7), and to Heaven and Hell: "It is finished!" (John 19:30) His blood was poured out. The New Covenant was sealed. The war was won. His Bride was redeemed. The Kingdom had come. Passover was fulfilled.

Jesus drank the fruit of the vine, the cup of the New Covenant in His blood, and then died. "For a covenant is valid only when men are dead" (Heb 9:16). We have come into our inheritance and have become co-heirs and co-rulers. We are now, this very moment, in the Kingdom. Do you *believe* it? Jesus fulfilled *all* that was written of Him.

Just as God made a covenant with Israel so the Israelites were set free on Passover to enter into the Promised Land, and did in fact enter into the Promised Land, so also, Jesus made a New Covenant with His people, so that they were set free on Passover to enter into the Kingdom, and as a result, His people have entered into the Kingdom.

Your access to everything in the Kingdom depends on *one* thing: *Belief.*

6

REGARDING THE LAW

It is possible there are some unanswered objections or questions about the New Covenant and the Law. I do not believe I can foresee all objections. I will address the objections I had to work out within myself, as well as the ones I have heard most often. Most commonly the objection comes in the form of defending the Law. Our non-spiritual worldview of "the Law" consists of the governing rules that are enforced by the police and courts. That concept is (either consciously or unconsciously) equated with a thing called God's Law or spiritual laws. All too often, "the Law" gets understood as "rules to live by" without stopping to consider the Jewish context and culture. It is helpful to understand the complexities of what Scripture writers were referring to when they used the term. Be willing to consider your understanding of "The Law" is at least incomplete.

The Torah and the Tanakh are the most common words used today among Jews when referring to the Scriptures. The Torah, or the Law is the first five books of the Bible. The Torah has a number of different names: the Law, the Books of

Moses, the Law of Moses, and sometimes simply, Moses. Bible translators have chosen to use "the Law" when translating "Torah" into English. Although the Law *most often* means the Books of Moses, occasionally, it includes all of Tanakh.[14] While The Torah consists of the Books of Moses, Tanakh is all of the Old Testament (for the Jew there is no New Testament). Tanakh includes the Torah, the Prophets, and the Writings (history, Psalms, and wisdom books).

The Ten Commandments and all other rules given to Moses at Mount Sinai are called the Mosaic Law. The Law [Torah] contains The Mosaic Law, which is first introduced in Exodus 18, then it is scattered throughout the rest of Leviticus, Numbers, and Deuteronomy with narrative and history sprinkled throughout. In order to clarify for the reader I will put a [Torah] after "the Law," like this: the Law [Torah] when needed to make a distinction between "law" and "Law." When the context is "laws and ordinances" the text will remain as is.

Most Christians do have the understanding that the Books of Moses are also called the Law [Torah]. Notwithstanding, when the modern Christian thinks of the Law [Torah], it often gets associated with a picture of an old man, with windswept beard, gray hair and two large stone plaques in hand, standing on a mountainous ledge. Even when we know intellectually that The Law and The Torah are synonymous, our working understanding is often simplified to the Ten Commandments. This idea has become prevalent despite its simplified and all too narrow definition. If pressed to expand their definition of the Law [Torah], Christians will often speak of the law found throughout Leviticus, Numbers and Deuteronomy yet fail to include Genesis and Exodus. To add to the confusion, when we

---

[14] In John 10:34 Jesus quotes from Psalm 82: "Has it not been written in your Law, 'I said, you are gods?'" Jesus referenced what He called "your Law" showing that the Hebrew understanding of "Law" is not exclusively the Torah but can extend to the whole of Hebrew Scripture [Tanakh].

read of "The Lord's commands" in the New Testament, it is almost always understood to be the Ten Commandments. If the Ten Commandments were what Paul meant in the following verse, he would surely be the most schizophrenic of all apostles: "Circumcision is nothing, and uncircumcision is nothing, but what matters is the keeping of the commandments of God" (1 Cor 7:19). Paul, who wrote Romans as a thesis on being dead to the works of the law and alive to the Spirit, was not suddenly arguing in favor of keeping the law. The "commandments of God" Paul was talking about are *not* the Ten Commandments. Rather, Paul was writing about the commands that God is speaking by His Spirit.

Because we have misunderstood what the ancient Jews (Jesus, the Gospel writers, Peter, James, Paul and others) meant when they spoke of the Law [Torah], we have interpreted the Bible through a Western-thinking, Gentile lens. We have neglected to acknowledge the Jewishness of its writers. If a Jew were to read the New Testament and come across the words "the Law" they would surely understand it as the Torah. They would get a different picture, far more panoramic, in their mind's eye. They would see a picture that encompassed everything from creation to the fall of man; to Noah, Babel, Abraham and the Patriarchs; to the journey into Egypt, Moses, the Exodus out of Egypt, and the wilderness wanderings; and to Joshua getting the anointing of Moses (Deut 34:9). We must remember that it was mostly Jews who wrote the New Testament. When Jesus spoke of the Law [Torah], and when Paul and others wrote of the Law [Torah], they had a Jewish worldview.

As you read the Bible, you will come across the "Law" (capitalized, i.e. Torah) and the "law" (not capitalized, i.e., a code of conduct), and you might not even realize the difference. Adding to the confusion, there is not always a distinction made in our English Bibles. While the New American Standard

Bible (NASB) uses capitalization, other translations do not. In those instances, it becomes very difficult for the reader to discern the meaning!

Understanding the difference between the Torah and the Mosaic Covenant is crucial. A few Scriptures are commonly used by conservative churches to validate keeping a connection with the Mosaic Covenant. We will go through these Scriptures and look at them in context. However, you must retrain yourself to understand "the Law" as the Torah. As you read Scripture, note the context in which the word "law" is used. As the word *is* interchangeable, context remains of the utmost importance. Clues in the text include capitalization. "Law" indicates the Torah rather than a singular "law". Context is everything. "The Law and the Prophets" can only be read as, "the Torah and the Books of the Prophets." Even so, we will see that in some passages "the Law and the Prophets" is narrowly defined by some to mean "Mosaic Law" with "the Prophets" getting lost in translation.

As stated earlier most Christians do have an understanding that there is a new law, and a new way to live, but they just can't justify the next step of leaving the Old Covenant altogether. Many of us have been taught, "The Law is a tutor to lead us to Christ." Based on that verse in particular (Gal 3:24), you can find evangelistic training tools and manuals on how to lead someone to Jesus using the law, specifically the Ten Commandments. Personally, I disagree with that particular method of evangelism, because its foundation was built on an incorrect definition of Law [Torah]. I believe that verse has been woefully misunderstood and I will show you why. In part, the misunderstanding comes because of our tendency to think of "the Law" [Torah] as the laws and ordinances given at Sinai. Evangelists will think to themselves, "If the Bible is true, the Law is a tutor which leads us to Christ, and the law is the Ten Commandments, then how do I revamp my understanding to align with God's truth?" It's an honorable motive to be sure, but unfortunately one that is based on a faulty premise. The result is a program on how to use the law or, in truth, the Ten Commandments to show someone their need for a Savior. The program usually goes something like this: *There was only ever one perfect man. You are not perfect. Have you ever stolen anything? Yes? Well, that makes you a sinner. Only Jesus was perfect, only Jesus was good enough to go to heaven. Therefore, ask Him to be your Savior.* Thus, the foundation has been laid for a works-based religion, coupled with a method of control. (More explanation is provided in the subsection, "The Law is God's Perfect Standard?") I will not deny that some have had success by using these methods. To that, I simply say that God will not leave Himself without a witness. He is after your heart, and He loves you.

The verse would take on an entirely different meaning, understanding and ultimately conclusion if you read it like this, "[the Torah] is a tutor to lead us to Christ." Jewish converts to the Way (Acts 24:14-15) understood this: the Torah was a teacher with Jesus hidden on every page and in every unrolling of the scroll. The Torah begins and ends with imagery of Jesus. In the first words of the Torah, we read "Let there be light" (Gen 1:3). It is in the reading of John that we discover that the light is Jesus. "In the beginning was the Word and the Word was with God and the Word was God ... He is the Light of men ... John came to testify about the light ... the light that was coming into the world" (John 1).

In the twilight of the last few verses of the Law [Torah], we again see the foreshadowing of Jesus in the life of Joshua (Jesus and Joshua are the same name, one anglicized from Hebrew, one from Latin). The very last verses of Deuteronomy 34 tell us that Moses has died, and now the nation looks to Joshua. Joshua, filled with the Spirit, became the commander of the army to lead the people into the Promised Land (Deut 34:9).

From first to last, from creations first light to Joshua, the Law [Torah] whispers the name of Jesus.

Let us look at the verse about the Law [Torah] being a tutor to lead us to Christ in a couple different versions. Galatians 3 reads differently in the NASB than in other more modern translations. The NASB, and also the Orthodox Jewish Bible, say exactly what the Jewish converts understood; the Torah tells the story of Jesus.

The NASB reads this way (pay close attention to the capitalizations or lack thereof):

> Is the Law [Torah] then contrary to the promises of God? May it never be! For if a law had been given which was able to impart life, then righteousness would indeed have been based on law. But the Scripture has shut up everyone under sin, so that the promise by faith in Jesus Christ might be given to those who believe. But before faith came, we were kept in custody under the law, being shut up to the faith which was later to be revealed. Therefore the Law [Torah] has become our tutor to lead us to Christ, so that we may be justified by faith (Gal 3:21-24).

The Orthodox Jewish Bible (OJB) reads a little differently. As you read, be aware of the article (the) before Torah, which would indicate *The Torah* (i.e., The Books of Moses) whereas Torah without the article indicates a singular law or rule.

> Is the Torah, as a result against the promises of the Lord? God forbid! For if Torah had been given that had the power to affect regeneration, then to be justified with God would indeed have been based on the eternally binding ordinances of the Torah. But the Holy Scriptures consigned all things under sin, that the promise might be given by faith in Rabbi, King Messiah Yeshua to the Believer.

But before faith came, we were being held in custody, being confined and guarded for the about-to-be-revealed faith. This is the result: the Torah functioned as our governess to lead us to Messiah, that by faith, we might be justified by the Lord.

Do you see "the Torah" leads us to Jesus? The Torah gave us hints and clues of Messiah, what He would do, where He would come from, etc. Our part is to use the faith given to us, in whatever measure, to put those clues together and conclude that these shadows were of the man Jesus. The Torah uses the stories of Abraham and others to show that faith in God and His promises make you righteous. Now extend that faith to the fulfillment of the promises found in Jesus. Now that Jesus has come it is faith in Him that makes one righteous. With the Torah finding fulfillment in Jesus, "We are no longer under a tutor" (Gal 3:25). The Torah shows us what to look for, what He will be like, etc. We are no longer looking for Messiah using the clues of a future-forward prophetic lens. We do not need that particular tutor to tell us what He is *going to* accomplish. We have history to look back upon. We can know with absolute clarity that Messiah came and He fulfilled the Law [Torah] and the Prophets. This is precisely why we are no longer under the tutelage of the old way of learning.

NOT ABOLISH, BUT FULFILL

The one other major objection to completely discarding the law (in favor of a new and better) is that Jesus "came to fulfill the Law." The unspoken understanding here is that if Jesus fulfilled the law, we ought to as well. He absolutely did fulfill the Law [Torah]. However, we should look at the whole verse in context:

> Do not think that I came to abolish the Law [Torah] or the Prophets; I did not come to abolish but to fulfill. For truly I say to you, until heaven and earth pass away, not the smallest letter or stroke shall pass from the Law [Torah] until all is accomplished (Matt 5:17)

The Gospels use this word "fulfill" several times. "Fulfill" and its variations is the Greek word *pleroō*, which means to make replete, or *finish (a period or task)*.[15] Of the 36 times *pleroō* is used, 35 times it is immediately juxtaposed to prophecy that is being fulfilled. Below is a sampling.[16]

> Then what had been spoken through Jeremiah the prophet was fulfilled (Matt 2:17).

> He left for the regions of the Galilee, and came and lived in a city called Nazareth. This was to fulfill what was spoken through the prophets: "He shall be called a Nazarene" (Matt 2:22b-23).

> In their case the prophecy of Isaiah is being fulfilled, which says, "You will keep on hearing, but will not understand; You will keep on seeing, but will not perceive" (Matt 13:14).

> And He began to say to them, "Today this Scripture has been fulfilled in your hearing" (Luke 4:16).

> I do not speak of all of you. I know the ones I have chosen; but it is that the Scripture may be fulfilled, "He who eats My bread has lifted up his heel against Me" (John 13:18).

---

[15] Spiros Zodhiates, *The Complete Word Study Dictionary: New Testament* (Chattanooga, TN: AMG, 1993), 1176-1177.

[16] The one exception is Matthew 3:15 where Jesus says to John, "Permit it at this time; for in this way it is fitting for us to fulfill all righteousness."

Matthew records Jesus' declaration that He had come to fulfill the Law [Torah] and the Prophets. After His resurrection, Jesus expanded on that thought in two different passages found in Luke 24. The difference between Matthew and Luke was that Luke was not a Hebrew. He was a Greek. Luke made sure his Greek audience knew Jesus fulfilled all prophecy concerning Him in Tanakh (the entirety of Hebrew Scripture).

> And He said to them, "O foolish men and slow of heart to believe in all that the prophets have spoken! Was it not necessary for the Christ to suffer these things and to enter into His glory?" Then beginning with Moses and with all the prophets, He explained to them the things concerning Himself in all the Scriptures (Luke 24:25-27).[17]

The above was spoken to the two men on the road to Emmaus the day Jesus rose from the dead. A few hours later, He repeated Himself to the remaining disciples in the upper room:

> Now He said to them, "These are my words which I spoke to you while I was still with you, that all things which are written about me in the Law of Moses and the Prophets and the Psalms must be fulfilled." Then He opened their minds to understand the Scriptures, and He said to them, "Thus it is written, that the Christ would suffer and rise again from the dead the third day, and that repentance for forgiveness of sins would be proclaimed in His name to all the nations, beginning from Jerusalem" (Luke 24:44-47).

---

[17] The Orthodox Jewish Bible translators give cross reference texts for a sampling of the prophecy that Jesus fulfilled in the Law and Prophets. "And having begun from Moshe Rabbenu and from all the Neviim, he explained to them in all the *Kitvei Hakodesh* the things concerning himself" (Luke 24:47). Cf. Gens 3:15; Num 21:9; Deut 18:15; Isa 7:14; 9:6; 40:10, 11; 53; Ezek 34:23; Dan 9:24; Ps 22; Mal 3:1.

It is undeniable Jesus came to *fulfill the prophetic words* written of Him in the Law of Moses, the Prophets, and the Psalms. It is also a distortion of Scripture to say something like: "Jesus came to live a perfect life according to the law (meaning the Ten Commandments) because we couldn't." *You will never find that backed up by Scripture.* That does not stop the distortion from being taught throughout Christendom. Try doing a search on the internet: "What does it mean that Jesus fulfilled the law?" You will find page after page affirming He did not break the Ten Commandments. The false teaching that the way Jesus fulfilled the Law [Torah] was by keeping the Ten Commandments minimizes His entire ministry, and completely misses the point. The only one who *could* fulfill the Law [Torah] was Jesus the Messiah, not because He was perfect and sinless, but because all prophecy in the Law [Torah] was *about Him.* The belief that we ought to fulfill the law because Jesus, our example, did unwittingly sets up the believer on a path toward works and shame rather than belief and abiding trust. Jesus did not ask us to follow the law, He asked us to follow Him.

Now draw your attention back to what was stated earlier:

> You must retrain yourself to understand "the Law" as the Torah. As you read Scripture, note the context in which the word "law" is used. As the word *is* interchangeable, context remains of the utmost importance. Clues in the text include capitalization. "Law" indicates the Torah rather than a singular "law." Context is everything. "The Law and the Prophets" can only be read as, "the Torah and the Books of the Prophets." Even so, we will see that in some passages "the Law and the Prophets" is narrowly defined by some to mean "Mosaic Law" with "the Prophets" getting lost in translation.

For too long, the words "Do not think that I came to abolish the Law or the Prophets; I did not come to abolish but to fulfill" have been used as a chain to keep believers in submission to the law. Instead, Jesus was saying this: "It's Me! Here I Am, Messiah, the One you have been waiting for! I Am the fulfillment of everything you have been waiting for! I have come to set you free, to conquer sin and death, to take you as My bride and bring you into the Kingdom of God!"

Since Jesus came to fulfill prophecy in the Law, what were some of those prophecies? Here is a small sampling: He is the seed of the woman who crushed the serpent's head (Gen 3:15). He is the seed promised to Abraham (Gen 22:17), and the sacrifice, of which Abraham prophesied when he was about to sacrifice Isaac on the altar (Gen 22:8). Jesus is the Passover Lamb (Exod 12:3), the Scapegoat (Lev 16:10), the ruler to whom the scepter belongs (Gen 49:10), the manna from heaven (Exod 16:4), the rock that provided water in the wilderness (Exod 17:6), the bronze serpent that healed those who looked to it (Num 21:8), and "the Prophet like Moses" who was to come (Deut 18:15).

He also fulfilled the Tanakh, not just the Torah, but the Psalms and the Prophets as well. One somewhat unknown example is found in a short chapter of Zechariah. Zechariah 3 tells the story of Joshua the high priest who takes away the iniquity of the land in a single day. (Recall that Jesus is the anglicized version of Joshua.) In this chapter Joshua is called the Branch, a known term for Messiah.[18] Another example that most of us are familiar with is Jonah. Jonah is a prophet who "dies" or goes down to the depths for three days and nights. On the third day, he is "resurrected," preaches the Word of God to a Gentile nation so that they receive salvation.

These prophetic shadows of Jesus, of His death and resurrection on the third day, "according to the Scriptures" (and sal-

---

[18] Jer 23:5; Isa 4:2; Isa 11:1-5; Jer 33:15-16; Zec 6:12-13.

vation being proclaimed to the Gentiles) became the heart of Paul's message. It is frequently quoted in Sunday worship services (Matt 12:17-21):

> For I delivered to you as of first importance what I also received, that Christ died for our sins according to the Scriptures, and that He was buried, and that He was raised on the third day according to the Scriptures (1 Cor 15:3-4).

Jonah is one foreshadowing of the three-day death and resurrection. Abraham going on a three-day journey to sacrifice Isaac is another (Gen 22:4). It is in the reading of Hebrews that we get a little more clarity, "Abraham reasoned that God could even raise the dead, and so in a manner of speaking he did receive Isaac back from death" (Heb 11:19).

Hidden within Genesis 1 is yet another foreshadowing of a resurrected life on the third day. Consider that life first appeared on day three. Three days out from complete darkness, God said, "Let there be [life]" (Gen 1:11-12). Prophetically, the life that was created on day three had a secret hidden inside of its DNA. Day three saw the creation of all "plants yielding seed" (Gen 1:11). A seed is used as parable and allegory of a picture of death and resurrection. Jesus and Paul both used the imagery. Jesus was resurrected on the third day after His crucifixion; heaven and earth's darkest day. The Branch, the seed, Jonah, and Isaac's pardon are all shadows, and the fulfillment, the complete picture, is Jesus.

After His resurrection, Jesus appeared to His disciples in the upper room. The same way He had appeared to the two disciples who were on their way to Emmaus, He talked with the remaining disciples, He ate with them and opened their minds to understand the Scriptures.

> He said to them, "This is what I told you while I was still with you: Everything must be fulfilled that is written about

me in the Law of Moses, the Prophets and the Psalms."
Then He opened their minds so they could understand the
Scriptures. He told them, "This is what is written: The
Messiah will suffer and rise from the dead on the third day,
and repentance for the forgiveness of sins will be preached
in his name to all nations, beginning at Jerusalem. You are
witnesses of these things. I am going to send you what my
Father has promised; but stay in the city until you have
been clothed with power from on high" (Luke 24:44-49).

It was fifty days later that Peter stood up on the Day of Pentecost and gave his famous sermon recorded in Acts 2. Surely,
the Scriptures that Jesus used just two months earlier were
burned into Peter's heart and soul. Having just received the
Holy Spirit and power Peter addressed the crowd. Undoubtedly, Peter used the same Scripture which Jesus had used when
he began to teach those who gathered. Why improve on perfection? The following is from Peter's sermon; in it he quotes
from Psalm 16.

> But God raised Him up again, putting an end to the agony
> of death, since it was impossible for Him to be held in its
> power. For David says of Him, "I saw the Lord always in
> my presence; For He is at my right hand, so that I will not
> be shaken. Therefore my heart was glad and my tongue ex-
> ulted; Moreover my flesh also will live in hope; Because
> You will not abandon my soul to Hades, Nor allow Your
> Holy One to undergo decay. You have made known to me
> the ways of life; You will make me full of gladness with
> Your presence" (Acts 2:24-28 [Psa 16:8-11]).

These are just a few examples of how Jesus' death and resurrection fulfilled the Law [Torah].

The death and resurrection was not the only prophecy Peter
counted fulfilled. Peter considered himself as living in the days

of the fulfillment of all the prophets from Samuel to Malachi. After Peter and John heal a cripple at the Beautiful Gate, Peter makes another public address. Empowered by the Holy Spirit, he declares, "And likewise, all the prophets who have spoken, from Samuel and his successors onward, also announced these days" (Act 3:24).

There are thousands of prophetic shadows of the Messiah. The shadows are meant to be pictures to encourage belief in Jesus. The Books of Moses teach us what to look for in the persona of "The Seed of Woman." All His mysteries and strengths are hidden in the pages. The Holy Spirit is waiting to reveal the hidden treasures to those who would seek Him. Yes, the *"Law is a tutor to lead us to Christ,"* and it does so beautifully when you know what you are looking for—evidence that Jesus is the Messiah.

NATIONAL LAWS

The Old Covenant and its laws were given to the nation of Israel. Abraham was given the promise of the land. One branch of his family had grown to include Jacob, Leah and Rachel; Jacob's concubines; all of Jacob's children and their spouses; and Jacob's grandchildren. It was a family around seventy strong. They were a large family, but even very large families don't have official laws. After Jacob's family had lived in Egypt 400 years, the seventy had multiplied to the number of a small nation. The Exodus from Egypt turned them into a sovereign nation, which requires some form of governing laws. They were a nation birthed in a day. They were not another Egypt; no, this nation belonged to God.

What sort of laws would they have? Every sovereign nation has a system of government and laws. When God rescued Israel out of Egypt and set them up as an independent nation, He gave them a system of government entirely unknown in the world. First, He appointed prophets and judges to rule the nation. The succession of leaders would not be by force or birth, but instead, by divine appointment. It was a thing unheard of. Think of it: what nation has rulers appointed by God?

Second, He gave a system of laws for daily living, work, and laws that provided assistance for the poor (don't cut the corners of the fields, harvest the field once only, leave the rest for the widows, orphans and strangers to glean; instruction for alms-giving, etc). Israel was the first nation with laws that considered the poor and those in need and *proactively* made provision for them.

Third, it was a system of morals and public behaviors. All these are contained in the Mosaic Covenant. In addition to being a covenantal contract, these laws and ordinances were to be the governing laws of the newly birthed nation of Israel. Deuteronomy 4 speaks to this:

> See, I have taught you decrees and laws as the Lord my God commanded me, so that you may follow them in the land you are entering to take possession of it. Observe them carefully, for this will show your wisdom and understanding to the nations, who will hear about all these decrees and say, "Surely this great nation is a wise and understanding people." What other nation is so great as to have their gods near them the way the Lord our God is near us whenever we pray to him? And what other nation is so great as to have such righteous decrees and laws as this body of laws I am setting before you today? (vv 5-8)

I have already stated reasons why the Mosaic Covenant has no hold on us. Here is yet another aspect to the truth that we are not under the Law of Moses: We are not the nation of Israel.

We are not living in the ancient nation of Israel. Requiring someone to follow ancient Israel's laws would be akin to requiring an American to also obey the laws of England. At one time New England was under the sovereignty of the English monarch. Now America is a new nation. Should American's continue to obey the laws of England? How silly! Nobody in America believes they are supposed to live by English rule *and* American laws. Yet that is the very thing some of the children of the Kingdom of Heaven believe when it comes to the laws of earthly Israel (Gal 4:24-26). Some would hold onto the old, because it is good in part. I am not denying the good within the old; I am saying the new is better.

SIN AND LAW

Many times the Apostles Paul and John say that we are not guilty according to the law, because there is no law.

For the Law [Torah] brings about wrath, but where there is no law, there also is no violation (Rom 4:15).

For until the Law [Torah] sin was in the world, but sin is not imputed when there is no law (Rom 5:13).

The sting of death is sin, and the power of sin is the law (1 Cor 15:56).

But if you are led by the Spirit, you are not under the Law [Torah] (Gal 5:18).

Whoever abides in Him does not sin (1 John 3:6-7).

Law and sin are tied together. The Law [Torah] was meant to bring about righteousness, but instead it brought about sin.

I would not have come to know sin except through the Law [Torah]; for I would not have known about coveting if the

Law [Torah] had not said, "You shall not covet" (Rom 7:7).

All of Israel had the Law of Moses, and because they were guardians of the Law [Torah] and righteousness, they were supposed to know how to pursue righteousness. God had met with them in real ways; they knew of and had seen the glory of the Lord. The Jews had oral tradition, the Scriptures, family stories, and personal interventions of the Divine in their history. In the story of the Hebrew nation, God Himself had defined sin, transgression, and abomination. The Gentile nations on the other hand had no such divine knowledge or intervention—not even close.

On Pentecost, when Peter preached to the crowds of Jews and Jewish converts (Acts 2), he called attention to the sin of the nation. The sin was rejecting the Messiah and handing Him over to godless men to be crucified. In Acts 3 Peter again preaches to a crowd of Jews with the same message: You sinned by requesting the death of Messiah. Repent, so God will forgive you and refresh you.

In Acts, the words of only a handful of sermons were recorded, seeming to indicate especially powerful or important truths. Peter preached the first two messages, these are in Acts 2 and 3. He quoted Scripture *as proof of who Jesus was* and called them to repentance for the particular sin of *denying the Messiah.* When the audience was Jewish, you can see the same elements: proof of the Christ and a call to repentance for denying Jesus as Messiah. Intriguingly, an astonishing thing happened when the audience was Gentile. Paul's message to the Gentiles was drastically different from Peter's message to the Jews. As much as the Jews are chastised and called wicked for not recognizing Messiah, the Gentiles *barely* heard about sin in the messages preached to them. Paul did not quote Scripture (at least not directly). Perhaps even more surprising is the realization that Paul quoted a *pagan* poem to reach his Roman audience for Jesus! When Paul gave his famous message in Athens, "The Sermon on Mars Hill," he did not chastise the Athenians for being sinners, call them wicked, or rebuke them for following other gods. Paul knew his audience, and his audience did not know—nor did they care— about Jewish law and the covenant the Jews made with God one thousand years or so prior to Rome. They were proud Romans, and the Mosaic Covenant meant absolutely nothing to them. Here is the whole message to the Gentiles in Athens. Read it again for tone and content, realizing the audience.

> Men of Athens! I see that in every way you are very religious. For as I walked around and looked carefully at your objects of worship, I even found an altar with this inscription: to an unknown god.
>
> Now what you worship as something unknown I am going to proclaim to you. The God who made the world and everything in it is the Lord of heaven and earth and does not live in temples built by hands. And he is not served by human hands, as if he needed anything, because he himself gives all men life and breath and everything else. From one man he made every nation of men, that they should inhabit the whole earth; and he determined the times set for them and the exact places where they should live. God did this so that men would seek him and perhaps reach out for him and find him, though he is not far from each one of us. "For in him we live and move and have our being." As some of your own poets have said, "We are his offspring." Therefore since we are God's offspring, we should not think that the divine being is like gold or silver or stone— an image made by man's design and skill. In the past God overlooked such ignorance, but now he commands all people everywhere to repent. For he has set a day when he will judge the world with justice by the man he has appointed.

He has given proof of this to all men by raising him from the dead (Acts 17:22-31).

We see this message was not calling down conviction for idol worship, or convincing the audience that they were sinners in need of a savior. He did not list the Ten Commandments as evidence that they fell short of God's perfect standard. Instead, he simply told them that God was devising their lives so they would seek Him and find Him because a day was coming when He would judge the world in justice. If the Apostle Paul, the author of Romans, did not use the "Romans Road"[19] as an evangelism formula, *should we*?

After a display of the power of God, Acts 14 records the short sermon spoken to the Gentile audience. Paul and Barnabas had healed a man, and the Roman citizens wanted to worship them.

> Men, why are you doing this? We too are only men, human like you. We are bringing you good news, telling you to turn from these worthless things to the living God, who made heaven and earth and sea and everything in them. In the past, he let all nations go their own way. Yet he has not left himself without testimony: He has shown kindness by giving you rain from heaven and crops in their seasons; he provides you with plenty of food and fills your hearts with joy (Acts 14:15-17).

The message of Good News to the Gentile audience was, "God has shown you kindness!" The kindness and reality of a powerful God who loves you *really is good news*!

Another biblically-recorded message to the Gentiles occurred when Peter spoke to Cornelius' household. They were

---

[19] The Romans Road is a series of Bible verses from the book of Romans (3:23; 6:23; 5:8; 10:13; 10:9-10). It is a memory device for Christians to present the Gospel message to unbelievers.

quite familiar with Jewish ways and customs. In the evangelistic message at Cornelius' home, Peter brings out this point (similar to the Athenian message of Paul): Jesus, the one they have heard about in signs and miracles, also judges the world and forgives sins. Contrasted with the Jews at Pentecost, Peter does not call the Gentiles at Cornelius' house "sinners."

> I now realize how true it is that God does not show favoritism but accepts men from every nation who fear him and do what is right. You know the message God sent to the people of Israel, telling the good news of peace through Jesus Christ, who is Lord of all. You know what has happened throughout Judea, beginning in Galilee after the baptism that John preached— how God anointed Jesus of Nazareth with the Holy Spirit and power, and how he went around doing good and healing all who were under the power of the devil, because God was with him. We are witnesses of everything he did in the country of the Jews and in Jerusalem. They killed him by hanging him on a tree, but God raised him from the dead on the third day and caused him to be seen. He was not seen by all the people, but by witnesses whom God had already chosen—by us who ate and drank with him after he rose from the dead. He commanded us to preach to the people and to testify that he is the one whom God appointed as judge of the living and the dead. All the prophets testify about him that everyone who believes in him receives forgiveness of sins through his name (Acts 10:34-43).

Today we have departed from telling the Good News that Jesus is King, Lord of Heaven and Earth; those who abide in His Kingdom receive healing, forgiveness and love. Instead, the Romans Road or following order of evangelism has been adopted: You are a sinner; sinners deserve death; Jesus came to give you the gift of life, He died instead of you; if you believe this, say a prayer so you will be forgiven and live forever. But if you don't accept His forgiveness, you are going to hell.

Of course that is over-simplifying the modern evangelistic message, but over-simplified or not, it bears no resemblance to the way the earliest Christians preached the Good News of the Kingdom. Neither does it parallel anything remotely close to what Jesus told His disciples to do. His methods were far more radical than most dare attempt. Most of our ways depend on our own intellect and ability. His ways depend on the Power of God and absolute faith in Him. When Jesus sent his disciples out to preach the Good News, He gave these instructions:

> And as you go, preach, saying, "The kingdom of heaven is at hand." Heal the sick, raise the dead, cleanse the lepers, cast out demons. Freely you received, freely give (Matt 10:7-8).

There is nothing in this message about hell, sin, or condemnation. Heaven itself witnesses to the world the Good News that the Kingdom is here, and Jesus is the King who has conquered all. How did we get so far away from the biblical model of trusting that Heaven would validate its own authority? Perhaps it started when His children stopped abiding, lost connection with the head, and in the vacuum of the Spirit's power, came up with a program.

The Law [Torah] was never, ever intended to be a battering ram to convict someone of guilt! Its purpose, if it even has one in the Gentile world, is most certainly not to measure oneself against God's perfection and our failures. What needs to be made clear is the Law [Torah] is an intensely beautiful, gloriously magnificent paintbrush that paints an intriguing yet incomplete picture of the full and astonishing glory we know to be Jesus.

> *He is the image of the invisible God, the*
> *firstborn of all creation. For by Him all things*
> *were created, both in the heavens and on*
> *earth, visible and invisible, whether thrones or*
> *dominions or rulers or authorities—all things*
> *have been created through Him and for Him.*
> *He is before all things, and in Him all things*
> *hold together. He is also head of the body, the*
> *church; and He is the beginning, the firstborn*
> *from the dead, so that He Himself will come to*
> *have first place in everything (Col 1:15-18).*

THE LAW IS GOD'S PERFECT STANDARD?

In yet another attempt to exalt behavior over faith, some may have been taught that the law is God's perfect standard!

This means that you must be able to follow all the commands of the Old Covenant.

Perfectly.

Your whole life.

Never failing.

Not once.

Ever.

(We already know we cannot).

But …

But, *if* we could, Oh! Glorious day!

If we did this, we would be "good enough" to get to heaven.

You know what all this is? Rubbish. Lies. Fantasies and fairy stories!

Even *if* someone kept all the laws and ordinances given to Moses, he still would not be "good enough" to go to heaven. In the same way that sinning is not *the cause* of someone going to hell, being "good enough" (i.e. following the Mosaic Covenant perfectly) does not grant you access to the Kingdom. Those who have access to the Kingdom do so because the Holy Spirit is alive in them. There is no neutral territory where a soul can stand. A soul is either in the domain of darkness or in the Kingdom of Heaven. If you are in the Kingdom, it is because He has rescued you. "For He rescued us from the domain of darkness, and transferred us to the kingdom of His beloved Son" (Col 1:13).

There has been a false idea implanted in the church that if a sinner continues in sin, then *for that reason*, he will go to hell. It usually sounds something like this, "If you keep drinking you'll go to hell" or any other number of various sins. "If you continue to [fill in the blank] like that, you will go to hell."

That is just not true.

You cannot adjust your actions to get *out* of hell. In the same way you cannot adjust your actions to go to heaven. So why, oh why, do we tell people that *if* they sin, they are going to hell? Right out of the starting gate, a foundation for a works-based Gospel had been laid, whether recognized or not. Heaven and Hell have been presented as a reward or punishment based on our *behavior*. The very idea that Heaven is somehow accessed by behavior is contrary to what Scripture teaches. Rather, the truth is the Kingdom is accessed by *faith*.

Many Christians are taught to try to rein in sin and sin less. On the surface, this sounds great, but it couldn't be more wrong. Jesus is not impressed with behavior modification. Less sin does not equal more righteousness. Faith equals righteousness; seeking Him in faith has always been the means to the Father's pleasure and rewards. We pursue righteousness by faith, not by changing our actions. Modified behavior in one's own strength equals a Pharisaical and a religious spirit. He asked us to abide in Him. If we abide in Him, *He*—not *me*—is doing a transforming work where sin reduces in direct proportion to our abiding in Him.

Only Adam had the "option" to sin and receive death. Nobody else gets the same "option." Adam and Eve were the only ones with the Living Spirit of God in them at "conception." Today we are born into the image of Adam, rather than the image of God (Gen 5:1-3). God did not create us, like He did Adam and breathe His Spirit into us. The reason people are perishing is because they lack the God-breath. We took on Adam's image after Adam lost the Spirit of God. Adam could not pass on what he did not have. People are not perishing because of something they are *doing*. People are perishing for no other reason than they just *are*. It would be so much better to tell someone, "Jesus is the Conquering King, the Lord of Heaven and Earth. With Him you have an inheritance as a co-heir of His Kingdom. It has been lovingly supplied by your Heavenly father, because He loves you. God has awesome, incredible things for you."

It surely is *good news*!

The Bible does not teach that the laws given to Moses are the way to righteousness. To the contrary, the Law [Torah], the Histories, the Psalms and the Prophets all testify to men and women who sinned according to law, yet were declared righteous before God. Abraham, Tamar, who seduced her father-in-law; Moses, Rahab the prostitute, Gideon, Samson, Jephthah and David. The list goes on and on. The singular testimony concerning every righteous man and woman is that they were *faithful* (Hebrews 11; Romans 4) as opposed to law-abiding. So why do well-meaning teachers put so much merit into keeping the law rather than living faithfully? Dare I postulate that one can be measured outwardly while the other cannot? I cannot measure the degree of your faithfulness to the Spirit's instruction within you. I can only know the conviction of Truth within myself.

Look at Rahab, the Canaanite prostitute from Jericho. She was an *active* prostitute and she was not from the tribe of Israel, yet the testimony from her mouth was one of faith in God: "I know that the Lord has given you the land" (Josh 2:9). So there she sits enthroned forever with the saints in the Hall of Faith, "Rahab *the Harlot*" (Heb 11:30).

King David knew he was a righteous man because he was in tune with the heart of the Father. David knew that it was God who made him righteous. He wrote songs about having a pure heart. Scripture called him a man after God's heart. God loved David so much that He promised David that the Messiah would come from his lineage. However, two of the commandments are: "You shall not murder" and "Do not covet another man's wife." Of course, you know the story about Uriah (a faithful friend to David). The story tells of how David coveted Uriah's wife, got her pregnant and had Uriah murdered. If anyone broke this so-called "standard of perfection," it was David. He did not just kill in self-defense; he murdered people just because he could. Read 1 Samuel 27. The list of killing is quite long. So long, in fact, that God told David, "You have shed much blood and have waged great wars; you shall not build a house to My name, because you have shed so much blood on the earth before Me" (1 Chr 22:8). David's indiscretions against the law were varied and many. Luckily for us all, God does not measure anyone's righteousness by their ability to keep the law. He was looking at David's heart (1 Sam 15:7), just as He is looking at yours. Surely, it is your heart's desire to follow Him.

It may surprise some to hear that the law as "God's perfect standard" is not taught or mentioned in the Bible. If you do not believe me, go seek it out yourself. I know it is difficult to adjust to new information, especially when it goes against a previously held belief. However, I am telling you the truth. This teaching has been inferred by a misapplication of what the Law [Torah] is and a misunderstanding of the word "perfect." Supporters of this teaching use a few verses to back this "perfect standard" idea. One such verse is, "The Law [Torah] is a tutor to lead us to Christ."

The reasoning goes like this: Christ was perfect and without sin, He fulfilled the Law. In addition, "The Law of the LORD is perfect, refreshing the soul" (Ps 19:7). The Law or, Commandments lead us to Christ by showing us our imperfection in light of His perfection. If we are to be transformed into His image, we should strive to fulfill the law, too. Fortunately, we already know the flaw in that logic. We have looked at the Law as a tutor, and yes, *the Torah* is perfect. Nevertheless, the *Old Covenant* has fault in it.

The truth is, if God measures us by any standard of righteousness at all, the standard He uses is Jesus. Through faith in Jesus, we absolutely measure up. "Now apart from the Law the righteousness of God has been manifested, being witnessed by the Law and the Prophets, even the righteousness of God through faith in Jesus Christ for all those who believe" (Rom 3:21).

> Yes, everything else is worthless when compared with the infinite value of knowing Christ Jesus my Lord. For his sake I have discarded everything else, counting it all as garbage, so that I could gain Christ and become one with him. I no longer count on my own righteousness through obeying the law; rather, I become righteous through faith in Christ. For God's way of making us right with himself depends on faith (Phil 3:8-9 NLT).

Nevertheless, this "perfect standard" teaching has been taught in some fellowships.

What. A. Burden.

That is just what the Pharisees did: they tied up heavy burdens and laid them on men's shoulders (Jesus, commenting on the Pharisees Matt 23:4). "But some ... Pharisees ... stood up, saying, '... direct them to observe the Law of Moses'" (Acts

15:5). Peter rejected the counsel of the Pharisees and questioned them, "Why do you put God to the test by placing upon the neck of the disciples a yoke which neither our fathers nor we have been able to bear?" (Acts 15:10).

There is nothing in the Mosaic Covenant that expects "perfect" adherence to the laws. On the contrary, there are steps to take within the covenant when you fail to follow the law, such as sin offerings. Yom Kippur is the holiest day provided for in the Law [Torah] it is also called the Day of Atonement. On Yom Kippur the priest made the appointed sacrifice and the sins of the people were forgiven (Lev 16:29-34). In the Old Testament, God did not seek out men and women who were perfect. God was consistently seeking out hearts that followed after and trusted in Him. God counted those people as righteous. Proverbs teaches that a man is seen as righteous even if he falls, for it is what he does *after* the fall that determines whether a man be righteous. "A righteous man falls seven times, and rises again" (Prov 24:16).

However, one must take note that on different occasions, under anointed leaders, Israel enjoyed and lived in the blessings promised under the Covenant. If someone is to take the stand and say, "The Law is God's perfect standard, and Jesus was the only one who was able to follow it," they must be ready to explain why, at various times within the history of Israel, the people enjoyed the *blessings* promised when they did follow the law. If the premise is true that nobody can follow the law, by extension it must also be true that the Jews were *never* able to realize the blessings, and were *always* under a curse. Yet, the Bible assures us that Israel and individuals occasionally *did* keep the commands of the Covenant.

> For he clung to the Lord; he did not depart from following Him, but kept His commandments, which the Lord had commanded Moses (2 Kings 18:6, regarding King Hezekiah).

> Yet you have not been like My servant David, who kept My commandments and who followed Me with all his heart, to do only that which was right in My sight (1 Kings 14:8).

> Then the Lord raised up judges ... Yet they did not listen to their judges ... They turned aside quickly from the way in which their fathers had walked in obeying the commandments of the Lord; they did not do as their fathers (Judg 2:16-17).

> Before him [Josiah] there was no king like him who turned to the Lord with all his heart and with all his soul and with all his might, according to all the Law of Moses; nor did any like him arise after him (2 Kings 23:25).

The blessings of the Covenant were realized under Joshua and his contemporaries, Gideon, David, Solomon, Hezekiah, Josiah, and others because they followed the law. Nevertheless, God was not looking for faithfulness toward the law; He always has been looking for faith in Him.

In the New Testament, Romans repeatedly pounds the point that it is faith that makes one righteous. The Bible is consistent throughout; every person who was said to be righteous had *one* thing in common, faith. They were not sinless. However, their faith *was* indicated by their behaviors. But do not get that confused with behavior being indicative of faith. The faithless Sadducees" and Pharisees" *behavior* was impeccable.

Why use the measurement of perfection? One possibility is a misapplication of the word "perfect." Biblically, perfect means "complete" (having all components necessary), or maturity (like wine coming to maturity) it does not carry the idea of "flawless." This is why different translations flip back and forth between perfect and complete. The rich young ruler of

Matthew 19 and Luke 18 asks, "What do I lack?" implying in-completeness.

> The young man said to Him, "All these things I have kept; what am I still lacking?" Jesus said to him, "If you wish to be complete, go and sell your possessions and give to the poor, and you will have treasure in heaven; and come, follow Me" (Matt 19:20-21 NASB).

The NIV chose a different definition and "complete" got trans-lated as "perfect." Without thinking much about it, the reader is given the suggestion of *sinlessness*:

> "All these I have kept," the young man said. "What do I still lack?" Jesus answered, "If you want to be perfect ..." (Matt 19:20-21 NIV).

Sometimes the above verse is used to back up the idea that God wants us to be perfect. Then it is often then coupled with, "Be perfect as your heavenly father is perfect" (Matt 5:48). This should really be rendered "become perfect."

"Be perfect as your heavenly father is perfect," comes at the end of a long sermon given by Jesus about the intent or spirit of the law. It is not a new and more restrictive standard than the law. The context for this command to be perfect/complete was Jesus correcting an oral tradition. The oral tradition corrupted the intent of the Old Covenant. In Matthew 5, Jesus says, "Be perfect [complete]." First, He corrected the wrong teaching that said, "love your neighbor *and hate your enemy.*" God never gave the instruction to hate one's enemy. Next, He expounded on what it means to *love your neighbor:* "Love your enemy and pray for those who persecute you." Remember, "Love your neighbor" is the only carryover law from the Old to the New.

But, seriously? Jesus wants us to be *as perfect as* our Heav-enly Father? Not if you define perfection as one who never sins. Not if you define perfection as one who follows the Ten Commandments, or the law. That is not the perfection God is looking for. He is actually looking for something quite different. On the other hand, if you define perfection as, "being complete, and lacking nothing," then, yes. In that case, yes, we are to be perfect. This is what we are right now: complete and perfect. Jesus has already made us perfect. He has made us that way, and so we are.

> By this will we have been sanctified through the offering of the body of Jesus Christ once for all … For by one offering He has perfected for all time those who are sanctified (Heb 10:10, 14).

> By this, love is perfected with us, so that we may have confidence in the day of judgment; because as He is, so also are we in this world (1 John 4:17).

> His divine power has given us everything we need to experience life and to reflect God's true nature through the knowledge of the One who called us by His glory and virtue (2 Peter 2:3 The Voice).

It is done. He did it. We are perfect(-ly complete), since now in Christ we have the Holy Spirit.

The last proof-text I found for this idea that the law is God's perfect standard is from James. "But one who looks intently at the perfect law, the law of liberty, and abides by it, not having become a forgetful hearer but an effectual doer, this man will be blessed in what he does" (Jas 1:25). I used to have a problem with James. I felt he was legalistic, so different from the freedom expressed by the other New Testament writers. I now realize it was not James. It was me. I had mistakenly read "law" through my own understanding of the Ten Commandments. I had been reading James as a New Testament holdout to the Old Covenant. I saw him as a preacher of works. Yet, a careful reading reveals he knew and understood the New Covenant, for he says, "If, however, you are fulfilling the royal law according to the Scripture, "You shall love your neighbor as yourself," you are doing well" (Jas 2:8). Royal law is most literally "kingly law" (as in, the law of the Kingdom). Additionally, this James is the same James in Acts 15 who stood up among the disciples and made the final decision that the Gentiles ought not to be made to follow the Law of Moses. This decision was guided by the Holy Spirit. No, the Gentiles are not required to follow Jewish covenantal laws.

James knew what he was talking about. It was I who did not understand James. James mentions "the perfect law that gives freedom" twice (Jas 1:25; 2:12). If Scripture is to interpret Scripture, then the conclusion is that the New Covenant is "the perfect law which brings freedom." Second Corinthians 3:17 says the *new law* is of the Spirit, and "where the Spirit of the Lord is, there is freedom." When James used the words "the perfect law," he was not talking about the Old Covenant Law. He even clarified what law he was talking about "the *perfect law* that gives freedom." James is talking about the New Covenant. Remember, the Old Covenant was *not* perfect- it had fault (Heb 8:7).

When James asks me to be a "doer" of the law, the command is to love, just like Jesus told us, "Love one another as I have loved you." So when the poor man comes to your meetings, do not give him the place on the floor. Love him, as Jesus would. I now believe the point James was making is that faith is a verb. It does *something*. Just like Jesus, love does something; it does not sit idly on its hands watching as a world of hurt goes by.

Therefore, when the assertion is: "The law leads us to Jesus as a schoolmaster in order to show us our failures, when we compare ourselves to a perfect God and His perfect law," the assertion is false. If you wish to see how thoroughly entrenched in our culture this falsehood is, a simple search on the internet of "God's perfect standard" will yield all the evidence you need. Most often, the search results will return, "The Ten Commandments are given to humanity to teach us our need for a Savior."

I do not wish to criticize anyone's ministry, so I will not name names or ministries. After all they are "fully convinced in their own minds," as I am in mine. Today, I am fully convinced that I will never again accuse someone of sin based on Jewish laws. Additionally, I will trust the Holy Spirit to be a powerful influence over the affairs of His beloved. I will trust *Him* to convince and convict of sin. It is my desire to tell *Good News*. Good is defined by *good*. The church has had to completely redefine good in order to say, "Have you heard the Good News? The Good News is you are a sinner and you are going to Hell, but ..." This tactic was never once used by Jesus, nor Paul, nor Peter, nor Phillip, nor John the Beloved. The Good News they preached is the Kingdom has come, and with it, its Victorious King (Acts 8:12).

I have already talked much about what the Law [Torah] is; a "Standard of Perfection" is not one of them. That idea is not even biblical. The Old Covenant law was *faulty*. It was *not* perfect. Therefore it *never could be* "God's perfect standard."

> *We are ministers of the New Covenant which is written not on stone, like Moses' law, but written by the Spirit. This New Covenant brings life. It is not like the Old Covenant that brought death even though it was glorious. Now, the Spirit with His New Covenant brings freedom. We look upon the glory of the Spirit, and we are transformed into higher levels of glory (2 Corinthians 3, Author's paraphrase).*

7

WHAT DOES THE
HOLY SPIRIT SOUND LIKE?

W hat *does* the Holy Spirit sound like? Some pastors and teachers do a great job teaching on this topic. Yet others prefer not to venture into this area at all. Nobody denies the existence and working of the Holy Spirit. It is just that He is a great unknown in some circles; trying to define Him proves quite elusive. In those circles where He is largely unknown, He has been downplayed from *fully* God to a willing Assistant. It is taught that He is the one who ignites a person's heart and soul to receive salvation, helps us as we read our Bibles and listens to our prayers, after that does little more.[20] Yes, He does all those things and also, insurmountably, so much more.

His voice is real, and His presence is part of the New Covenant Jesus made with us. Jesus said, "the Holy Spirit, whom the

---

[20] If you are unfamiliar with the Holy Spirit, I recommend the book by Francis Chan, *Forgotten God: Reversing Our Tragic Neglect of the Holy Spirit* (David C. Cook: Colorado Springs, CO: 2009).

Father will send in My name, He will teach you all things, and bring to your remembrance all that I said to you" (John 14:26).

He is God. He is the most powerful force in the world today.

He lives within you, and if you willingly partner with Him, He will do great and wonderful things through you. The Holy Spirit lives within us. He writes His laws on our hearts and puts them on our minds. He has a voice and an opinion, so it is crucial to know His voice and to be able to discern it over all others. Indeed, we do hear all sorts of voices. Our own, our mothers, fathers, our piano teachers telling us to sit up straight or our football coaches telling us to keep our heads up. Those who have influenced us, for good or bad, remain in our memories long after their physical presence is gone. We hear and remember very clearly the voices of the world as well as those of the spiritual realm. Unfortunately, sometimes, the Holy Spirit is not as loud as we wish He would be.

HE IS LOVING; NOT ANGRY

It is fundamental to know within your heart, mind and soul that His voice is loving, and kind. God is always good. His primary motivation is always love. Some church traditions teach that God is angry with sin and by extension angry with sinners. Know this: there is great danger in believing God is an angry God. If you believe He is angry, you will never accurately discern the voice of God.

The discernment between the Holy Spirit and the voice of the Accuser comes in the same way any other discernment would come. Were someone I love to give me constructive criticism, I would accept it, because I would have faith in the heart behind the criticism. If, however, a person with whom I have no relationship gave the same criticism I would probably be offended. The differences between the two situations are found in tone and heart attitude. Of course, the tone of the words is a form of communication in itself; tone sets the stage for the content of the words. Heart attitude is the motivation behind the words. Know that His heart is always for you, not against you.

> If God is for us, who is against us? He who did not spare His own Son, but delivered Him over for us all, how will He not also with Him freely give us all things? Who will bring a charge against God's elect? God is the one who justifies; who is the one who condemns? Christ Jesus is He who died, yes, rather who was raised, who is at the right hand of God, who also intercedes for us. Who will separate us from the love of Christ? Will tribulation, or distress, or persecution, or famine, or nakedness, or peril, or sword? Just as it is written, "For Your sake we are being put to death all day long; We were considered as sheep to be slaughtered." But in all these things we overwhelmingly conquer through Him who loved us. For I am convinced that neither death, nor life, nor angels, nor principalities, nor things present, nor things to come, nor powers, nor height, nor depth, nor any other created thing, will be able to separate us from the love of God, which is in Christ Jesus our Lord (Rom 8:31-39).

God is always for you. Sometimes the words may be difficult to hear, but they are always framed in love. They give calm and peace to your soul. The enemy of your soul is just that, your enemy. He cannot even try to be kind. It is just not in him. He may quote the Bible to you. Using Scripture is an astonishingly good tactic; yet consistently, *Scripture in the mouth of the Enemy still brings failure, death and condemnation.* Condemnation is not conviction. Do not ever equate the two.

Condemnation means a damnatory sentence.

Conviction means full assurance, most certain confidence.

If we have conviction before God, it is most certain confidence. We have so much confidence that we know we can enter the throne room of the king with full rights as sons, always, *no matter what.*

Do you know the heart of Father toward you? It is love. God is love. He is always going to love you. He loves you and calls you His son. He adopted you into His family because *He wanted you to be in it.* You did not sneak in through the back door. He was waiting for you to look toward Him. As soon as you gave one glance, one thought, one inclination His way, as far as He was concerned, it was all over! The pursuit was on; He pursued you with the greatest love the universe will ever know. Angels are still in awe of it.

If you believe that God is motivated by anything other than love, I cannot possibly hope to fully sway you to the idea that God is always good and His voice is always love, in such a short time. I can only alert you to the dangers of believing that He is not.

God is not angry with you. If you believe He is angry, that gives the Enemy a wide-open door to mock, condemn, chastise, and pour on the guilt. You will accept the voice of the Enemy as the voice of God, because you are already under the belief that God is angry. Mockery and condemnation are the language of anger. You will try to do better and sin less, but the condemnation never stops. The mockery is never satisfied because you are not even hearing the voice of the Holy Spirit. Many have left the faith because they've concluded that there is no satisfying this angry, vengeful and wrathful God. You've tried to be good, and still the voice inside never changes, always demands more, and is never satisfied (just like the grave, death and destruction; see Prov 27:20, 30:16).

Only God can speak to us in a way that produces real change. The following passage from 2 Corinthians is a fantastic

measure to weigh godly sorrow (which is sent by God and produces change) against worldly sorrow (which brings death):

> I knew you would be upset with my last letter, but I do not
> regret sending it. If there were times I did have second
> thoughts, it was because I could see that the letter did hurt
> you, even if only for a while. Now I am glad—not because
> it caused you grief but because you were moved to make a
> permanent change that can happen only with the realization
> that your actions have gone against God—I'm glad to
> know you suffered no long-term loss because of what we
> did. Now this type of deep sorrow, godly sorrow, is not so
> much about regret; but it is about producing a change of
> mind and behavior that ultimately leads to salvation. But
> the other type of sorrow, worldly sorrow, often is fleeting
> and only brings death. Look at what is happening among
> you! Notice how authentic and diligent you have become
> because this godly sorrow has been at work in your com-
> munity. But there's more: your desire to clear your name,
> your righteous anger, your respect, your longing, your zeal,
> and your concern for justice. All these demonstrate how
> you have been made clean. So when I wrote my last diffi-
> cult letter, it was not to comfort the victim or confront the
> perpetrator—it was to stir up your sincere devotion for us
> under God's watchful eye. In the midst of all that has hap-
> pened, though it has been difficult, we are comforted and
> encouraged. When we saw the relief and joy on Titus's
> face, we celebrated even more because his spirit had been
> totally refreshed by you (2 Cor 7:8-13 The Voice).

Yes, Godly sorrow produces change while worldly sorrow
only brings death.

If you believe that God loves you with an everlasting love,
that He is pleased with you, that He wants good for you and
calls you up to a higher level of knowing Him, then the lan-

guage of love is *easily* discerned from the language of anger. When we abide with the Holy Spirit, He points out our short-comings, and we see sin for what it is, we leave the sin in our past and never look back. On the other hand, when the Enemy points out our sin, we become self-focused, full of self-loathing, and feel worthless. It is a mournful sorrow that only looks at the damage and never gives hope for a future with a different outcome. This is the death Paul speaks about above. When God does the correcting, you focus on Him. You feel empowered by grace to move forward, only to look back when there is a lesson to be learned, and not to repeatedly kick yourself for being a fool. You will have a sense of grace and assurance that somehow God will take care of it. You will have a new resolve and confidence that if the situation arises again, you already have a plan to confront the issue or respond differently.

The hellfire-and-brimstone preachers wonder why so many fall away after evangelistic campaigns in which a God of hellfire and anger is preached. Perhaps the answer lies in the God they are preaching. God is not angry at us. God loves us. What kind of disconnected God would He be if He couldn't decide if He were angry at me for sinning and is sending me to hell, or that He loves me so much He is willing to die for me? Furthermore, the LORD of Heaven's armies, the Creator of the Universe (who *already knows* what I am going to do), vacillates between states of anger and love depending on my daily actions.

That's. Just. Crazy.

That is not the God I know. My Jesus does not talk to me in anger. He does not talk to anybody in anger. It is His kindness that leads us to repentance (Rom 2:4). The voice of anger and condemnation do not lead to repentance, only to death, and that voice belongs to another.

Ask yourself, "Does the voice I hear align with His character?" When He tells you what to say, how to act, how to respond, what to do in any given circumstance, it will always look like love. That does not mean it is always easy. Sometimes love is a difficult choice. Regardless, it will always look like Him. He is a rock, a firm foundation. He does not change like shifting shadows.

He is and will always be creative, powerful, faithful, loving, kind, good, merciful, filled with emotion, and in pursuit of a relationship with you. No matter what *we* do, *He* continues to pursue the relationship.

HE IS SEEKING

Behold, the Lord's hand is not so short that it cannot save; Nor is His ear so dull that it cannot hear. But your iniquities have made a separation between you and your God, and your sins have hidden His face from you so that He does not hear (Isa 59:1-2).

This is one of those verses in the Bible that gets quoted way too often, and nearly always out of context. The Bible says this just once. It was only after generations of constantly breaking covenant, spiritual adultery of worshiping other gods, and right before Israel was taken into Assyrian captivity. Even then, God was pleading with them to return to Him. The whole Bible is the story of God making a way for something called atonement. At onement. At one-ment, being "at one" with. Yes, that is what it means. Jesus made us one with him, and we cannot be separated. Even in the very beginning in the Garden, the all-knowing God (who knew very well what Adam and the woman had done) did what He had always done: He came down to meet with them in the cool of the day. It was Man who hid and therefore separated himself from God, not God who withheld

His presence from Man. He has always been the one seeking mankind.

Adam hid among the trees. I do not know where Israel "hid," but once again, it was *their* sin that made them hide from God. God was not separating from them. He sent prophets to call them back to Him. The Good News is even though the chapter starts with Israel's sin and separation from God, by time you get to the end of Isaiah 59, God has made a way for atonement. It starts with God grieving over the separation; then segues into what life has become without Him. Finally, God presents the solution in the last verse. The beautiful wondrous solution is one only a loving Father seeking at-one-ment with His children, could possibly dream up. *"And as for Me,"* says the Lord, making what follows His responsibility and His alone.

> "And as for Me, This is my covenant with them," says, the LORD; "My Spirit which is upon you, and my words which I have put into your mouth, shall not depart from your mouth, nor from the mouth of your offspring, nor from the mouth of your offspring's offspring," says the LORD, "from now and forever" (Isa 59:21).

Their sins had separated them from God, so God made a New Covenant to never be apart from His children again. Only a God who is love could conceive plan like that!

HE IS LIFE

So how do we discern the voice of the Holy Spirit? First, it is loving. Second, there is life in His voice. There is freedom and comfort in the voice. It does not look back in hopelessness but soothingly assures you of a better future. Much has been said about the fruit of the Spirit (Gal 5:22-23), and what it looks like reflected in the life of the believer. You cannot bear His fruit without being like Him. Have you considered that these fruits are the very essence of the Spirit Himself? They are all good! Love, joy, peace, patience, kindness, goodness, faithfulness, gentleness, and self-control are all Him. These are the qualities of His character, therefore all these character traits will be heard in the sound of His voice. The voice of the Holy Spirit within you does not lapse into anger or anything else contrary to His character.

There is life in His voice. It brings out a desire to do good, and a previously unknown strength to do so.

> For the kind of sorrow God wants us to experience leads us away from sin and results in salvation. There's no regret for that kind of sorrow. But worldly sorrow, which lacks repentance, results in spiritual death (2 Cor 7:10 NLT).

The supernatural source of the strength and desire come out of God-produced sorrow. Even sorrow, when it originates in God, brings salvation. Because that is who He is; all life and every good thing flow from Him. In Him there is no darkness at all (1 John 1:5).

Often the strength comes from having a predetermined, different course of action before a situation ever arises. Repentance means changing the way you think about something. It does not mean *feeling* remorse. The sorrow that does not change the way you think about an issue is not from the Father. Neither does it bring life, only death. There is no regret in God-produced sorrow. "For the kind of sorrow God wants us to experience leads us away from sin ... there is no regret for that kind of sorrow." Repeat it until you believe it. God does not make you regret. Godly sorrow *leads* you; it leads you away from sin. God gently takes your hand and says, "This way, it's so much better, come on, you can do it, child. I believe in you."

That is the voice of kindness. That is life. That is your Father's voice.

If you are hearing the Holy Spirit, He may speak Scripture to you, but not necessarily.

If He is encouraging you to do something, you may argue with Him, but you know it is the right thing to do. For example, He may ask you to apologize to someone. That may be humiliating, but God is more interested in growing your character than nursing your pride. Admittedly, the truth is, you *know* it is the right thing to do and you just do not want to do it. You know it is the right thing, because there He is, writing His law of love on your heart. If you have already done something wrong, and He is speaking to you about it, His voice is still kind. If you hear anything after sinning which then causes you to hate, loath, or reject yourself, then you are not hearing the Holy Spirit. Yes, it is true that God hates sin. I hate cancer, but that does not mean I hate people with cancer. If you and I are able to differentiate between cancer and a person with cancer, how much more is God able to differentiate between sin and death, and His creation that He died for? He hates sin, but his voice is not angry. His voice brings life. Jesus said that the Enemy comes to steal, kill and destroy. Conversely, Jesus came to bring life, abundant life. When God speaks, life springs up from nothing. I do not think He can help it! He opens His mouth, and the word goes forth like rain showers in season and do not return without accomplishing what He desires (Isa 55:11).

HE IS EMPOWERING

Maybe His voice is not terribly loud or specific. Maybe it is not even words. Perhaps it is a prompting, but it will still "feel" right, even if you cannot explain it. It will be a pull toward, an inclination, a suggestion. He will allow you to *choose*. The choice comes through a gentle voice, a tug, or a strong urging, but not through a harsh demand. Remember when you were first saved? Did He *demand* you accept salvation? Was His voice harsh and angry then? Neither is it now. His voice has not changed. Unfortunately, it could be possible that you were taught about a God who continues the curses of the Old Covenant. Because of that you may have been listening for an angry voice. Glory to God, we are under a New Covenant in which all of our sins, and therefore the curse of sin, is completely wiped away.

Are you hearing contradictory things? That is not God either. God does not speak in contradictions. Do you feel immobilized, having differing ideas that cause you to have no clear direction? Contradiction is chaos, and God is not a God of chaos. He is a God of peace, and He will bring peace along with the answer you seek. Though I am broadening the context of 1 Corinthians 14:33 somewhat, it still stands that God is of peace and not confusion. His voice will give peace to your soul. There will be no conflict of "yes and no" or "stay and go" directives.

What if you are not hearing anything at all?

You have plenty of spiritual principles from which to work. Work from the context of what *is* clear. Which job should you take? ... Silence ... Perhaps He is giving you a choice. Sometimes there is a clear directive, and yes, sometimes He does care about the job. Other times, maybe He is leaving it up to you. We do have a free will, you know; sometime we tend to forget that reality when it comes down to it. Often we relegate our freewill to initially choose Him or not to choose Him. For some reason after salvation, we think we are supposed to be obedient in *everything* down to insignificant details. Our post-salvation total obedience really ought to be called what it is: "a brand new sort of bondage." We have spiritualized it and call it "knowing His will." Take this job or take that job. In the meantime, make disciples, pray for one another, feed the hungry, whatever your passion happens to be. Silence does not mean He is not with you nor does it mean He's giving you "the silent treatment" as if He were angry with you. Do not let it immobilize you. Do something, make a decision, and trust Him to correct your course if necessary. Keep your ear open to His voice, and when He speaks, listen. If you are not hearing anything, continue listening anyhow. Abiding in the silence, and being comfortable within it, is a lesson every mature lover of God has learned. The result is greater levels of faith and a deeper confidence.

You may have heard that if you set your compass off by just one degree, you will miss Hawaii by thousands of miles. You were not told the rest of the story. The rest of the story is the Holy Spirit is the pilot, and He is at the helm every minute of every day. When you abide in Him, you do not even have to set the compass.

He will get you there.

Guaranteed.

*But I tell you the truth, it is to your advantage
that I go away; for if I do not go away, the
Helper will not come to you; but if I go, I will
send Him to you ...*

*But when He, the Spirit of truth, comes, He
will guide you into all the truth; for He will not
speak on His own initiative, but whatever He
hears, He will speak; and He will disclose to
you what is to come. He will glorify Me, for He
will take of Mine and will disclose it to you. All
things that the Father has are Mine; therefore
I said that He takes of Mine and will disclose it
to you (John 16:7, 13-15).*

Made in the USA
San Bernardino, CA
04 April 2014